The View from the Cross

*Cycle B Sermons for Lent and Easter
Based on the Gospel Texts*

John W. Clarke

CSS Publishing Company, Inc.
Lima, Ohio

Library of Congress Cataloging-in-Publication Data
Clarke, John W., 1947-
    The view from the cross : Cycle B sermons for Lent and Easter based on the Gospel texts / John W. Clarke. -- 1st ed.
        p. cm.
    ISBN 0-7880-2664-X (alk. paper)
    1. Jesus Christ--Passion--Sermons. 2. Bible. N.T. Gospels--Sermons. 3. Lent--Sermons. 4. Lenten sermons. 5. Easter--Sermons. 6. Church year sermons. 7. Common lectionary (1992) I. Title.
    BT431.3.C57 2011
    252'.62--dc22

                                        2011015139

For more information about CSS Publishing Company resources, visit our website at www.csspub.com or email us at csr@csspub.com or call (800) 241-4056.

ISBN-13: 978-0-7880-2664-5
ISBN-10: 0-7880-2664-X   PRINTED IN USA

This collection of sermons is dedicated to the congregation of the First Congregational Church of Meriden, Connecticut, United Church of Christ. For nearly ten years they have nurtured, supported, and allowed me to preach, teach, sing, pray, and write as ministry with them. There are not adequate words to say a proper "Thank You" to them all! I hope that these sermons can communicate to them a proper "Thank You," for all that they have done and meant to me.

Table of Contents

Introduction   **7**

Ash Wednesday   **9**
Spiritual Discipline
Matthew 6:1-6, 16-21

Lent 1   **15**
Jesus and John at the Jordan
Mark 1:9-15

Lent 2   **21**
Expectations and a Cross
Mark 8:31-38

Lent 3   **27**
Cleaning the Temple — Cleansing Our Lives
John 2:13-22

Lent 4   **35**
God's Love and You
John 3:14-21

Lent 5   **43**
Life Lived in Glory
John 12:20-33

Passion / Palm Sunday   **51**
A View from the Cross
Mark 14:1—15:47

Maundy Thursday   **59**
The Perfect Example to Follow
John 13:1-17, 31b-35

Good Friday   65
From the Courtroom to the Cross — A King's Journey
John 18:1—19:42

Easter Day   73
The Gardens of Life
John 20:1-18

Easter 2   83
Should We Doubt Thomas?
John 20:19-31

Easter 3   91
What Is the Point?
Luke 24:36b-48

Easter 4   99
The Shepherd of Love
John 10:11-18

Easter 5   107
Are We Withering on the Vine?
John 15:1-8

Easter 6   117
Living a Joyful Life
John 15:9-17

Ascension of Our Lord   125
Reflections of a Healthy Church
Luke 24:44-53

Easter 7   133
A Time Between Time
John 17:6-19

Introduction

From Ash Wednesday, Maundy Thursday, Good Friday, Easter, Ascension, and finally the Seventh Sunday of Easter the Christian community walks with Jesus to glory. However, the journey itself is not so glorious. There are many unseen stumbling blocks along the way.

The sermons in this book reflect, I hope, the journey of faith that all of us must take as preachers, teachers, and fellow travelers along the way. There is good news to be discovered on our journey. There are some good and some not so good people who will travel with us. From time to time we may even find ourselves unsure if we are good or able enough to continue without help. At some point we may want to step off the well-traveled road and take stock of what it is we are doing. In other words, the life of our Lord will intersect with our own lives and that is a reason for joy but also reason for a detailed mental examination of our own feelings, thoughts, and motives.

So I invite you to participate in the sermons offered here. They are written for your enjoyment and with an eye toward a better understanding of what Jesus went through for our sake. The great hymn by George W. Kitchin says it best, "Lift high the cross, the love of Christ proclaim till all the world adore his sacred name."[1] How to do that in a sermon is the task of the preacher and the intent of this book.

— Rev. Dr. John W. Clarke

---

1. "Lift High the Cross," George W. Kitchin, Rev. Michael R. Newbolt © Hope Publishing Co. All rights reserved. Used by permission.

Ash Wednesday
Matthew 6:1-6, 16-21

Spiritual Discipline

"Ashes, ashes, we all fall down," that refrain from a children's song says much in terms of the way people now and in ancient times thought of ashes. There has always been symbolism to the way that ashes were used and at times displayed on the face, or the entire body. Even today we see pictures of tribal people covered in ashes as they celebrate or mourn an event.

In ancient Israel the symbolism of ashes was seen as a visual reminder of the human condition. The actual act of burning represented that which was no longer viable, that which once existed but was no more. This ancient symbol of abandonment and grief was adopted by the early church and when applied to the human body signified our own sinful condition. As we begin our Lenten journey, it is then appropriate that we use ashes as a sign that warns of the days ahead — days that will be filled with pain and grief but ultimately joy and glory.

Our gospel reading for this day is a rejection of Pharisaic practices. First of all Jesus speaks about the way that the Pharisees go about giving to those in need. He wants them to know that righteousness is not a matter between one person and other, but about a person and God. When you want to do something good for someone else, you do not and should not put on an act about how good you are because of what you are doing. You do it because it is the thing that a child of God should do for another child of God. There is no need for a great show and there is no need for you to try to convince people through your actions that what you are doing is anything other than an act of grace.

Lent provides us with a unique opportunity to see how important it is that we act in ways that are pleasing to God. The human drama of this time of the church year is undeniable, and it is that drama as it plays out that is important in our journey of faith, it is not important that we be the center of the drama, we are at best stagehands. True righteousness before God demonstrates an understanding that there is no reward in being good, except the reward of being good, and that is reward enough.

As most of you know Ash Wednesday often begins a time of giving up something. I want to center in on fasting as it has such a prominent part in the way we view ourselves and of what we think is really important in our lives. Fasting usually plays a pretty big role in how we interact with the season that is about to unfold for us all. The truth of the matter is that far too many people think this act of giving up or fasting is, well, an act! The reality is that giving up chocolate is not a sacrifice on the part of the one giving it up. Giving up eating meat every day or giving up scotch does not count! The whole idea in the act of giving or giving up something should come from the notion that giving up something would benefit not only yourself but, if not more importantly, would benefit someone else.

It is so important on this Ash Wednesday that we focus on exactly why and what the discipline of giving up is all about. Handing over something of yourself in order to find meaning in your journey of faith is a worthwhile endeavor. You can give money or some other material thing to someone in need and in so doing find real meaning as you recognize and focus in on the fact that what you are doing is being done for the glory of God. It is the same with fasting.

Throughout scripture fasting is referred to as the abstaining of food for spiritual purposes. It is not a hunger strike or a diet plan because each of these activities has with them a purpose that is not holy or spiritual. Fasting, if done the way scripture describes, is a very spiritual practice to aid one's spiritual life. Biblical fasting always centers on spiritual purposes.

The Pharisees made a big deal out of their fasting just as they did about giving to the poor. They loved fasting because it gave them another reason to show off. They thought that it made people see them in a more favorable light. They believed that when people saw that they were fasting, they would think that they were spiritually superior to the common folk. They were working hard to get people to notice them and in so doing, they hoped to gain in stature to the general public. They were wrong!

Moses, King David, Elijah, Queen Esther, Daniel, the apostle Paul, and Jesus Christ, all have one thing in common: fasting. Unfortunately the idea of fasting has fallen prey to our modern culture. When people think about fasting, they usually think about weight loss programs. Modern people need only turn on the television to see what I am talking about. In fact you don't really have to feel the hunger pains that come with fasting because in our world today there is very likely a pill to help you through the process without feeling too much pain.

Again, motivation becomes an important part of what you are doing and why. If you are fasting to impress yourself or anyone else, you are sadly mistaken in what you are doing. If that is what you are doing, you are no different than the Pharisees that Jesus was describing in our reading. He told them in no uncertain terms and is telling all of us that any motivation to fast should come from knowing that God can see what you are about and that should be enough.

In Luke's gospel, chapter 4, we are told that Jesus ate nothing for forty days and that when those forty days were over he was famished. There is instruction for fasting in scripture. The normal way to fast involved abstaining from all food solid or liquid, except water. In other words there was a genuine sense of being deprived and really having to struggle with keeping your fast without giving into temptation.

From time to time a debate about whether or not scripture commands fasting from the Christian will come up. Is it a requirement? Is it as much a part of the fabric of Christianity as the Lord's Supper or baptism? Although many passages deal with the subject of fasting, two stand out as important. Especially since they are teachings that come directly from Jesus. First, from our reading for today,

> And when you fast, don't make it obvious, as the hypocrites do, who try to look pale and disheveled so people will admire them for their fasting. I assure you, that is the only reward they will ever get. But when you fast, comb your hair and wash your face. Then no one will suspect you are fasting, except your Father, who knows what you do in secret. And your Father, who knows all secrets, will reward you.
> — Matthew 6:16-18 NLT

These verses seem to indicate that fasting is as much a part of the Christian life as giving and praying (the context of these verses). Jesus says, "when you fast." Not "if." Is Jesus then commanding us to fast? I really don't think so. I think Jesus was teaching a group of people who commonly practiced fasting. The Pharisees and many Jews had as part of their week, a fast. So, although Jesus said, "when you fast," He does not say "you must." Second,

> One day the disciples of John the Baptist came to Jesus and asked him, "Why do we and the Pharisees fast, but your disciples don't fast?" Jesus responded, "Should the wedding guests mourn while celebrating with the groom? Someday he will be taken from them, and then they will fast. And who would patch an old garment with unshrunk cloth? For the patch shrinks

and pulls away from the old cloth, leaving an even bigger hole than before. And no one puts new wine into old wineskins. The old skins would burst from the pressure, spilling the wine and ruining the skins. New wine must be stored in new wineskins. That way both the wine and the wineskins are preserved."

— Matthew 9:14-17 NLT

These verses say with clarity that the disciples would not fast while Jesus was with them, but they would after he was gone. In this passage, we see that Jesus upheld the practice of fasting and expected his followers to do this discipline after he had left them. Perhaps it is the word "command" that is messing us up. Jesus never commanded fasting. He did not say, "You shall fast." But he did expect that members of the kingdom of God would practice fasting. Should we as Christians fast? Yes.

Fasting must forever center on God. God asks the question, "Did you fast unto me?" (Zechariah 7:5). Our fasting must be done under God's direction and we must have our eyes fixed to him. Our one intention should be to glorify our Father in heaven.

Our actions should serve to remind us who and what sustains us. We should come to the conclusion that although we need food, food alone will not sustain us. Our journey of faith will need more strength than we can gain by eating or drinking alone. Colossians 1:17 says that "in Christ" all things hold together. By abstaining from food, one feasts on the word of God and is nourished by it. Fasting should bring balance to our lives. During this season we need to ask how and why we allow the nonessentials of life to take over. How often do we want things we don't need? How often do things other than God control us? Fasting helps keep the natural desires of our human selves in check and balances our spiritual selves.

The struggle for material possessions, which dominates so much of our lives, need not define our lives. As a follower of Jesus Christ we cannot let materialism dominate our lives. We have to work hard to seek the things that glorify God. The Christian should not allow an attitude of worry about what may or may not happen tomorrow characterize his or her life.

As we journey together into this Lenten and Easter season, we need to be sure that we are motivated to bring ourselves into a closer and more intimate relationship with our Savior. I say that because religious devotion is an intimate and deeply sincere relationship with God, and not meant to be some personal showcase for public display. We should never pay, give, or fast in order to look good. The only motivation we should be energized by is the energy that moves us to express our love and obedience to God in ways that bring glory to God and in so doing bring wholeness to the lives of all of God's children. Amen.

Jesus and John at the Jordan

Beginning in verse 9 Mark goes out of his way to communicate that Jesus quite literally went out of his way to seek the approval of John. Jesus understood that John was a well-established and important figure to the wider populace and receiving John's blessing would go a long way in Jesus himself establishing much-needed credibility. In a way, having John who was already recognized as God's prophet baptize him was a visible reminder to all that God would welcome all who came to be baptized. We can see just how important this action was. We see Jesus' actions certified when God descends as a dove and says, "You are my Son, the Beloved; with you I am well pleased" (Luke 3:22 NRSV).

In the final verse in today's reading we see that the age of God's eschaton has come and the journey into Lent and into the Easter season begins.

This gospel reading is all about the baptism of Jesus. This is one of the events that all three of the synoptic gospels (Matthew, Mark, Luke) describe and so was obviously an event that the early church saw as of great importance.

Mark's gospel gives us the facts, straight and clear but gives little else in terms of a description of the event. We must always remember that Mark is most concerned with communicating exactly what happened and is often brief on details. This is also one of the few instances where the great church historian Luke doesn't give us much more than

Mark, but Saint Matthew takes up the slack. In Matthew's account we hear:

> Then Jesus came from Galilee to John at the Jordan, to be baptized by him. John would have prevented him saying, "I need to be baptized by you, and do you come to me?" But Jesus answered him, "Let it be so now; for it is proper for us in this way to fulfill all righteousness." Jesus replied, "Let it be so now; it is proper for us to do this to fulfill all righteousness." Then he consented. And when Jesus had been baptized, just as he came up from the water, suddenly the heavens were opened to him and he saw the Spirit of God descending like a dove and alighting on him. And a voice from heaven said, "This is my Son, the Beloved, with whom I am well pleased."
>
> — Matthew 3:13-17 NLT

There is an ancient story that comes to us from the fifth century AD and it concerns Saint Patrick baptizing King Aengus. The baptism was by full immersion.

During the baptismal ceremony, so the story goes, Saint Patrick leaned on his sharp-pointed staff and inadvertently stabbed the king's foot.

After the baptism was over, Saint Patrick looked down at all the blood, realized what he had done, and begged the king's forgiveness.

"Why did you suffer this pain in silence?" Saint Patrick asked.

The king replied, "I thought it was part of the ritual."

In truth there just may be more to this little story than first meets the eye. People will often put up with a loss of comfort if they believe that doing so will bring about some sort of personal gain.

Scripture is pretty clear that John the Baptist had been doing all he could do to get people to come into the Jordan and in that act, finding the repentance they all so badly needed, even if they didn't know they needed it. One can just see the people gathering, listening, and wondering what this desert prophet was all about. Just what was he saying and exactly how was walking into the Jordan River going to accomplish what John promised?

The natural extension of this question would be to ask why on earth did Jesus find it necessary to go into the river to be baptized by John in the first place. I think the question we need to ask this morning is pretty clear and that is why Jesus needed to be baptized?

Was Jesus in need of repentance? For some people, even asking the question raises more questions than answers. In fact, for some people asking the question is about like questioning the validity of Jesus himself.

However, let us not forget that one of the most essential qualities of Jesus is his humanity. So the question is not out of place, it is just not needed. Jesus was without sin, period! That being the case, why did he go into the river to be baptized by John?

It is helpful at this point to look at the other accounts of this baptism. Much like the Christmas story we need the input of the other synoptic gospels to help us better understand what was going on here.

One of the things that stands out to me is that, at least initially, John himself did not think Jesus needed to be baptized. In point of fact, John thought Jesus ought to be baptizing him! "I need to be baptized by you, and do you come to me?"

It is pretty clear that John had the same question as all of us. He needed to understand why Jesus felt any need to be baptized at all. The answer to that question comes in Jesus' response to John's dilemma, "Let it be so now; for it is proper for us in this way to fulfill all righteousness."

What did Jesus mean? I think Jesus wanted John and all of those gathered on the shore to see and witness what was happening and in doing so learn that by coming to John in the River Jordan, Jesus was acknowledging the wonderful claim that God had on his life and through him in all of our lives.

In Jesus' submission to John the Baptist, we see a sign of the humanity of Jesus and his complete submission to God the Father. Jesus' visual submission gives us a visual picture with just as much importance as the picture of the dove descending while Jesus was still in the water.

All who witnessed this act could see that Jesus had taken a courageous stand by bringing himself into the everyday life of the shopkeeper, the farmer, and the shepherd. He was showing forth the grace of God to all who saw and then to all who heard what had taken place at the hands of John.

Jesus' example showed people that when they themselves took that walk into the waters of baptism, their lives would never again be the same. They would be changing the direction of their lives and in so doing would be clearing away the old life and bringing in a new one filled with hope and renewed possibilities.

In Jesus' submission to John in the river he showed just how much he loved God and just how much God loved him. As John poured the water on Jesus, all could see that Jesus was following the will of God in his life and that those who followed Jesus would be doing the same.

Indeed this demonstration of Jesus' devotion to the will of God conjures up images of another scene of submission and humility when at the Garden of Gethsemane, knowing that he was going to die on the cross, he prayed: "Father, if you are willing, remove this cup from me; yet, not my will but yours be done" (Luke 22:42 NRSV).

It was the ultimate submission to the Father's will — to go to the cross for our sakes — to reconcile us to the Father. But following the Father's will was painful.

But Jesus' baptism was more. It was also a way of Jesus announcing to the world that his ministry was about to begin. His baptism provides the portal through which his ministry begins to take shape. His baptism provides a consecration of his ministry and a visible reminder of what we all must do if we want to follow into that water and into the life that is promised in baptism.

Remember our account here in Mark is not the only time that we have heard some similar remarks about what God is thinking when we hear at the Transfiguration, "This is my Son, the Beloved; listen to him!" (Mark 9:7).

Growing up in the American Baptist church, baptism by immersion was the only choice one had. Although I have long been a member of the United Church of Christ, I have never forgotten that Jesus was baptized as an example for us, all of us.

By coming to the River Jordan and by submitting to John, Jesus gave us all a beautiful, clear picture of what it is we are to do ourselves if we choose to follow in Jesus' footsteps. He exemplified the words from Matthew 28:19-20, commonly called the Great Commission "Go therefore and make disciples of all nations, baptizing them in the name of the Father and of the Son and of the Holy Spirit, and teaching them to obey everything I have commanded you" (Matthew 28:19-20 NRSV).

Once again we remember God's response: "You are my Son, the Beloved; with you I am well pleased."

As we enter into Lent we would do well to apply to our own lives what we have been witness to in Mark's gospel for today. It is one of the shortest and yet clearest accounts of what we can do in order to be a part of the ministry of Jesus Christ our Lord. When we do follow Jesus from baptism to ministry both individually and as a church, we just may hear God whispering "with you I am well pleased."

It reminds me of a story from *Giants of the Missionary Trail* (1954) that Jonathan Goforth (1859-1936), the great Canadian missionary in China, used to tell. Jonathan's father put him in charge of one of the family farms at the age of fifteen.

He drew special attention to one very large field that had become choked with weeds. His father told Jonathan, "Get that field cleared and ready for planting. At harvest time, I'll return and inspect it."

Jonathan put a lot of time in plowing and replowing, sunning the deadly roots and plowing again until the whole field was ready for seeding.

He then went and procured the best seed for sowing.

When all was finished, Jonathan invited his father over to inspect the field. When his father arrived, Jonathan led him to a high spot from which the whole field of beautiful waving corn could be seen. Jonathan didn't say a word — he only waited for the coveted "Well done."

His father stood for several minutes silently examining the field for any sign of weeds but there were none. Turning to his son, he just smiled.

"That smile was all the reward I wanted," Goforth used to say, "I knew my father was pleased. So it will be if we are faithful to the trust our heavenly Father gives us."

Amen.

Expectations and a Cross

These verses from Mark's gospel are a call to commitment, a call to sacrifice, and a call to give up everything of earthly value in life. To say these are difficult verses is truly an understatement. It is pretty clear that the disciples are not at all ready for what Jesus is saying. They are not ready for Jesus to die and they certainly are not ready to die themselves.

We have to remember that the disciples are confused and frightened. They are still looking for Jesus to do something really spectacular but they are not ready to even contemplate what Jesus seems to be saying. They will understand the kingdom later, after the cross and after the resurrection. It is pretty clear that the disciples could not see what Jesus was talking about because they were looking for the wrong thing. How very *human* of them!

It may be beginning to dawn on the disciples that Jesus was not going to establish military rule. He was not going to be gathering an army and challenging the military and political establishment. He had not come to establish some sort of earthly messianic kingdom, at least not at that time.

Just a few verses earlier Peter had identified Jesus as the "Christ." However, Jesus himself had not told anyone to assign any title to him. Jesus was much more concerned with his mission than any earthly title, especially since titles seem to assume that the person with the special title is somehow different from everyone else. Jesus wanted to keep his humanity while at the same time helping people see that God had something much more important for him and for all of them to do. From this point on Jesus is traveling headlong into the journey that will take him to the cross, and from now on how his name is used will be determined by how Jesus himself speaks of himself and his ministry.

For example, the opening verse for today, "Then he began to teach them that the Son of Man must undergo great suffering, and be rejected by the elders, the chief priests, and the scribes, and be killed, and after three days rise again" (Mark 8:31 NRSV). This expression appeared only twice before in Mark's gospel. In both instances it was used to show the significance of an event for those early followers.

The title "Son of Man," especially suited Jesus' mission in its totality. The phrase is free of any political baggage, thus eliminating any false expectation that he was going to become politically involved in unseating the powers currently in control. At the same time the title is like one of his parables, as it leaves room for more than one definition. It combined all the elements of suffering and glory in a way that no other designation could. It served to combine different elements of who and what he was doing into one simple phrase, "Son of Man."

Our gospel lesson this day presents us with Jesus announcing in unambiguous terms what is going to happen to him in the days and weeks ahead. Lent is such a wonderful reminder of how we ourselves must take the journey with Jesus in order that we might better understand what it is that happened to him and what needs to happen to us today. Much like the disciples who were with him at that time, we also must be reminded of why Jesus came into the world and what it was that happened to change history as we know it.

When Jesus tells his followers what is going to happen, our good friend Peter steps up to the plate and says aloud what everyone else would say had they the courage. Peter in essence tells Jesus what he has said about himself must not be allowed to happen. When he does, he gets a response that could never had been anticipated, "Get behind me, Satan! For you are setting your mind not on divine things but on human things" (Mark 8:33 NRSV).

Peter was an unwitting spokesperson for Satan because he was reacting purely from a human point of view. We can't much blame him for that. How else could he react to such a statement from the man he thought would be his knight in shining armor? Peter did not know nor could he have known at this point in time that the way of the cross was God's way and Jesus would never abandon it.

There's the story of a soldier frantically digging in during battle as shells fall all around him. Suddenly his hand feels something metal and he grabs it. It's a silver cross. Another shell explodes and he buries his head in his arms. He feels someone jump in the foxhole with him and he looks over and sees an army chaplain. The soldier thrusts the cross in the chaplain's face and says, "I sure am glad to see you. How do you work this thing?"

In this scripture when Jesus talks about bearing our cross, we could ask the same question: "How do you work this thing?" Peter didn't know how to work or deal with the cross either. It has been said that the only reason Peter ever took his foot out of his mouth was to switch feet; it is here, at Caesarea Philippi, outside of Galilee in the shadow of Ancient Palestine, where Caesar was a god, that Peter discovered that a wandering carpenter from Nazareth, who was heading for a cross, was the Son of God.

There is hardly anything in the entire gospel story, which shows the sheer force of the personality of Jesus, as does this incident. It comes in the very middle of Mark's gospel and that's intentional, because this is the peak moment for Mark. The cross is the very heart of the gospel. A suffering Messiah who would die upon a cross had important implications for those who would follow him.

Jesus does not dance around the fact that if you witness what is going on and what will be going on in the days and weeks ahead and you still want to follow him, then you will have understood why all of this was necessary. So, he stated two requirements that will be needed in order to take up the cross and follow.

On the down side, one must deny self and say no to the ways of the world. Self-denial is not to lie about who you are; rather, it is the denial of "self" in turning away from the idolatry of self-centeredness and all attempts to orient one's life by the dictates of self-interest.

On the up side, although it does not seem to be the up side, one must take up his cross, saying yes to God and moving forward with your cross into the world. Cross carrying was not a common way of communicating something. It was not an established Jewish metaphor. However, the image of a man carrying a cross was a vivid picture of Roman-occupied Palestine. The image of a crossbearer brought to mind the sight of a condemned man who was forced to demonstrate his submission to Rome by carrying part of his cross through the city to his place of execution. To do that same thing, to carry the cross, was to publicly demonstrate one's submission and obedience to the authority against which he had previously rebelled.

In one way, this moment was a crisis for Jesus. Whatever the disciples might be thinking, he knew for certain that an inescapable cross lay ahead. The problem confronting Jesus was this: With the cross looming, had he had any effect at all on the disciples in the world at that time? Had he achieved anything? Had anyone discovered who he really was? If he had lived, taught, and moved amongst these men for three years and no one had glimpsed the Spirit of God upon him, then all his work had gone for nothing. There was only one way he could leave a message with people and that was to write it on someone's heart.

The truth is that those who follow Jesus must take up the cross, their own cross, not Jesus' cross. It does not mean suffering as Jesus did or being crucified as Jesus was. Rather, it means accepting the consequences of following Jesus without reservation for Jesus' sake and the gospel. For some this includes physical suffering and even death, as history has demonstrated.

When you look at the reading for today and put it into historical context, you can better understand why Jesus asked the question of his disciples earlier (v. 27) what people were saying about him. His disciples shared with him the popular rumors and reports. And having shared what people were saying about him, Jesus then asked them, "Who do you say that I am?" This is personal; it is very personal.

Suddenly, Peter realized what he had always known deep down in his heart. This was the Messiah, the Christ, the Anointed One, the Son of God. With that answer Jesus knew that he had affected people and made clear who he was.

There is another question we must answer, for no sooner had Peter made this incredible proclamation than Jesus told him he must tell no one. Why? Why could they tell no one who Jesus was? First and foremost, Jesus had to teach Peter and the others what being Messiah would mean both present and future. Because Jesus knew that his role as Messiah was not at all what had been anticipated by so many for so long.

Throughout their existence the Jews never lost sight of the fact that they were God's chosen people. They always regarded the greatest days in their history as the days of King David, and they dreamed of a day when another king of David's line, a king who would once again make them great in righteousness and in power, would arise.

Biblical history is clear that this dreamed-of greatness would never come about naturally through the passage of time. The harsh reality was that they came under Assyrian rule and Babylonian rule and Persian rule and Greek rule and

Roman rule. They began to believe that it wasn't likely that someone would simply rise up and make everything turn out the way they had always dreamed.

These are just a few of the reasons why Jesus used such penetrating rhetorical questions to show the supreme value of understanding how difficult the journey would be, but also that at the end of the journey was a new way of living, a new life that was eternal. Knowing that the journey would be long and hard Jesus says to them in verse 36, "For what will it profit them to gain the whole world and forfeit their life?" The answer is nothing, because having "gained the whole world" they have in the end irrevocably lost eternal life with God, with nothing to compensate for it.

The gospel for this Second Sunday in Lent, reminds us all that in the end those who follow Jesus, those who "take up one's cross," may fall short on their commitment at times. They have at least discovered that losing one's life in this age is a small price to preserve eternal life in the age to come. We must decide whether we want to come and be with our Savior, or whether we want to save our lives in the world, we cannot have it both ways. The cross means dying to this world and embracing the world to come. On this the Second Sunday in Lent, the question that all of us must ask is, "Which is it?" Amen.

Cleaning the Temple —
Cleansing Our Lives

Having heard the gospel this morning let me introduce a word from Paul when he said to the church in Ephesus, "And that Christ may dwell in your hearts through faith, as you are being rooted and grounded in love" (Ephesians 3:17 NRSV).

What Paul is saying here is the more Christians know about Christ; the more amazed we are at Christ's love for us. When Jesus lives in our hearts, we discover a love that goes right down into the soil of God's loving revelation and creation.

By extension then, if we allow that love to grow and become secure, we then become a dwelling place of God. Quoting Paul again, "Or don't you know that your body is the temple of the Holy Spirit, who lives in you and was given to you by God? You do not belong to yourself, for God bought you with a high price. So you must honor God with your body" (1 Corinthians 6:19-20 NLT).

The key to our gospel reading for this Third Sunday in Lent is the repetition of the idea concerning belief. It is so important in fact, that John uses the word "witness" no less than 27 times in his gospel. For John there is a single reason to witnessing and that is to force people to confront what they believe, or do not believe, and help them find the gospel that is Jesus Christ. That is always John's theme. In fact it is so important that he says in John 20:31 (NLT), "But these are written so that you may believe that Jesus is the Messiah, the Son of God, and that by believing in him you will have life."

John was especially impressed with the wondrous deeds that he himself witnessed. John not only saw miraculous things take place, he also knew those miracles were not done to make Jesus look like a "rock star" but rather they were performed as signs to manifest the true nature of the Christ who worked them.

In John we see a man who believed, followed, and changed. John entered into a new and personal experience with Jesus. John became more than just a friend, he became a personal witness who was so filled with the love of Jesus and the hope offered through that love that he had to tell others about it. His heart became so full, it had to be emptied!

John discovered that the very idea that Jesus lives in us is enough to make us want to get on stage and tell anyone who will listen all about him. I guess you can say that I myself am doing that very thing, right now! You see, the fact that Jesus Christ the Son of God would be humble enough to be in me is almost more than I can comprehend. If I were to go into the hospital and have an MRI it will not show the outline of a person living in me. The Bible reminds us that God is Spirit. You cannot touch Spirit, you cannot see Spirit, but you feel that Spirit within your very soul! How cool is that? To think that the God that created the universe and all that is in it lives in me, is present in me, and wants to live in the hearts of all creation is overwhelming.

In discovering this indwelling of the Spirit of God I find that I want to share with you some of that which I have been lucky enough to experience myself. Lent is a good time for the pastor to do some personal witnessing. In point of fact, it is a good time for all of us to do some witnessing. And I say that knowing it is an uncomfortable subject for many. For most folks in the more "traditional" churches this idea of witnessing is a bit foreign.

When we begin to understand that God loves us so much more than we can ever know, we just may begin to see why it is so important to become that temple of the Holy Spirit that Paul spoke of to the church in Corinth. Everything God is, God is to the fullest: God's love is 100% loving; God's gentleness and peace is 100% gentleness and peace. God is all the peace we need and God is by definition holy. But we should also remember that as much as God loves us, God hates that which separates people from God. In other words, God hates sin! God absolutely hates anything that keeps us away from God's presence in our lives. In the story of creation it is instructive to remember what words were spoken. God did not tell Adam and Eve that God thought they had been a little unorganized and perhaps a bit messy. God did not tell Noah to do the backstroke or tread water for a few days. No, God makes it clear that there are and will be consequences to sin. "For the wages of sin is death, but the free gift of God is eternal life through Christ Jesus our Lord" (Romans 6:23 NLT).

I think it is important that we understand God's disdain for sin. It was why Jesus hung on the cross. God's feelings about sin are pretty evident throughout this chapter of John's gospel.

One of the things that John's gospel portrays so well is that Jesus is in a sense a local commodity. The people Jesus are with and those with whom he is speaking have an idea of who he is and where he comes from. Most of them probably thought of him as Joseph's son, the kid from Nazareth. Others may have known him as a carpenter in his own right. However, Jesus had crossed a line and he was messing around in much more disturbing territory. We know that Jesus had already been to visit John at the River Jordan. He had already accepted John the Baptist's claim that he was the Son of God and now he had stirred the city up by booting all the moneychangers and cattle dealers from the temple. Just consider what is going on here.

John records the cleansing of the temple at the beginning of Jesus' ministry. Remember the other three gospels all have Jesus at the temple toward the end of his public ministry. John may well have been aware of what the other gospels contained but believed it was important to place the story early on as a way of highlighting the fact that Jesus attended the temple and he knew what was going on there.

The buying and selling of animals in and around the temple was common practice. The activity was probably seen as a convenience for the pilgrims who came to the Holy City for Passover. But as is often the case with unsupervised business (Wall Street, banking), abuses developed, and the people who were the consumers became the consumed! With money to be made, worship would soon take a backseat.

It is likely that Jesus did not protest the use of the temple in this way as it did help the pilgrims to be able to make a proper sacrifice. He was angry with the way in which it was being accomplished. He protested that the entrepreneurs who were operating in the temple were more concerned with profit than with the reason they had been allowed to do business there in the first place. This was the temple of God and as such it deserved better attention and respect. For the better part of his life, Jesus had been to the temple and watched those people pollute the house of God in the name of the almighty dollar instead of the almighty God. He was furious at their disrespect and greed. He was disgusted that the temple floor was soiled with animal feces and the smell of urine burned his nostrils. This was the place where people came to worship God, it was for them and for Jesus, God's house. The sin of the cheating moneychangers and the greed of those men broke his heart. So Jesus decided it was time for someone to clean the place up, and he drove them back out into the streets.

In an interesting use of words, John says that his disciples remembered that it was written, "Zeal for your house will consume me" Jesus showed forth his zeal (John 2:17). And just what is zeal? Zeal is passion, it is love on fire. It is a consuming dedication to a purpose. Jesus was passionate about God. He was passionate about purity. He was passionate about the things of God. Jesus was certain of one thing and that was that God doesn't dwell in filth.

You will remember that earlier I spoke about our hearts being God's dwelling place. For years people have prayed over and over that Jesus would work in their lives. Sadly for too many people it seems that they just don't feel that presence in their lives. It is likely that there is a very good reason for this, and what Jesus did at the temple may be a good instruction to us all as to what we have to do to prepare our temple to receive him. We ourselves must be sure to clean out the things that would hinder Jesus from entering into our hearts. We need to get the junk out and make room for the Spirit.

Some of you need to cleanse the temple. You need to get busy and clear it out, drive out the cattle, upset the moneychangers, and shovel out the dirt and manure that is keeping Jesus from working effectively in your life.

Lent is a time when we can and should examine our lives to see if there is any unclean thing there. Far too many of us go through our day, our week, our months, our years, and our lives without examining ourselves and letting Jesus examine us through his word. Our heart is like a garden and sin is as quick to pop up as the weeds. If we stop examining our lives and asking God to search us out, we will quickly be overcome with unwanted weeds. The Spirit doesn't dwell in dirty temples. As Jesus absorbs the sin, the ecstasy of the Spirit explodes within us. There is no shortcut to being alive in God; it comes as you confess your sin in silence. You need to go off by yourself. You need to give Jesus time to open the door to your heart. Lent gently urges us to ask ourselves when was the last time we were free of the things of the world long enough to allow Jesus to purify and cleanse us?

You may believe in the forgiveness of sins, but belief alone will not be enough. You can believe in the forgiveness of sin, but the question is have you come to terms with the fact that sin has taken up residence in your life? Have you surrendered, have you allowed Jesus to come in and do some cleaning? Have you let Jesus penetrate into our heart? Once again, Lent allows us a unique opportunity to ask the one who knew no sin, to take your sin away! Jesus wasn't crying in Gethsemane because of the pain, he wasn't crying because of the agony. He was torn because he knew he would take on all our sin.

Don't dwell on the sin you have confessed. We are all guilty of doing something to separate us from God in the past and then allowing that same thing to sneak back into our lives, take up residence, and once again set us apart from that which we all need: the love of God. Sisters and brothers in Christ if you have nailed your sin to the cross, the word says that God casts it as far as the east is from the west (Psalm 103:12). That is a long way. That says to us that when the sin is absorbed that which hides sin from our lives is no longer there. That sin, that thing, whatever it is that keeps us from walking hand in hand with Jesus into the Lent and Easter journey is finally identified and removed. Jesus has cleared away all that keeps us from living in comfort with the Holy Spirit.

If our separation from God is smothering the Spirit, if sin is a wet rag on the Spirit, it holds us back. Today I urge you to reach out to Jesus and allow him to take your hand and bring you to that place where the Spirit dwells. Reach out to Jesus and help him help you fill the cluttered spaces of your life and permeate those spaces with new life and new hope. When you do, you will begin to understand maybe for the first time that it is through the cross of Christ that the Holy Spirit fills you with the same zeal that filled our Lord. Allow that wonderful passion to grow within you. When you do, you will be able to walk into your future knowing that the Spirit of God dwells within you and you are once and forever the temple of God! Amen.

God's Love and You

Let's begin this Fourth Sunday in Lent with our gospel reading for today. I include the reading in the body of today's message as it begins in an awkward place following as it does on the heels of Jesus' telling us that no one except himself has ascended into heaven. In other words Jesus had been lifted up and it is with that in mind that we read from the New Living Translation the following:

> And as Moses lifted up the bronze snake on a pole in the wilderness, so I, the Son of Man, must be lifted up on a pole, so that everyone who believes in me will have eternal life. "For God so loved the world that he gave his only Son, so that everyone who believes in him will not perish but have eternal life. God did not send his Son into the world to condemn it, but to save it. There is no judgment awaiting those who trust him. But those who do not trust him have already been judged for not believing in the only Son of God. Their judgment is based on this fact: The light from heaven came into the world, but they loved the darkness more than the light, for their actions were evil. They hate the light because they want to sin in the darkness. They stay away from the light for fear their sins will be exposed and they will be punished. But those who do what is right come to the light gladly, so everyone can see that they are doing what God wants."
> — John 3:14-21 NLT

A visitor to Ystad, Sweden, tells of the little church located there. It is not a particularly beautiful church and is exceptional in no way except that when you go inside, you notice there is a crucifix hanging on the wall opposite the pulpit. The figure of our Lord is life-sized and lifelike even to the use of real hair mangled beneath a crown of thorns.

How did this unusual crucifix happen to be in a Swedish Lutheran church?

Well, it seems that in the early 1700s the King of Sweden paid an unexpected visit to the church. When the pastor saw the king in attendance he was overwhelmed. He ignored the text for that Sunday and replaced it with an oratorical outburst of tribute and praise for the king.

Soon afterward the church received the crucifix from the king. With it came this command: "Hang this within the church so that whoever stands in the pulpit will be reminded of his proper subject."

On this Fourth Sunday in Lent it will do all of us good to be reminded of the proper subject of this special season of the church year. We do not want to get ahead of ourselves here. It is so easy to fix our eyes on Easter and the entire Holy Week celebration that we miss how vital and important the weeks leading up to Holy Week are.

As a music director friend of mine is fond of saying, you cannot sing about the old rugged cross before that old cross has been put on the hill. It is important that we keep our eyes focused on the journey to the cross and the empty tomb, lest we miss so much that the rest of the trip loses its significance.

There is real power in the images presented in our lesson for today. The thought of being elevated toward heaven must not be dismissed out of hand. Further, it is just as important to recognize that the image of Moses raising that bronze snake on a pole is a visual reminder that this action on the part of Moses signals to the people a cure for the punishment due them for disobeying God. The visual image being communicated to Jesus' followers of Jesus being lifted up on cross for the sin of the people is in a very real, powerful, and personal way, telling the people to look to the cross. It is a reminder that the cross represents a cure for the punishment they must be free themselves from for the sins they have committed.

That is powerful imagery.

As the weeks in Lent unfold and we draw nearer to the cross, it is only human to lean more and more toward that old rugged cross. We know that without that cross we will not get to the glory of Easter. We see in our lesson from John's gospel, a summary for the cross. John is giving us in this lesson the reason why Jesus died. It is the reason why the king of Sweden thought that the proper subject of any preacher is the death and resurrection of Jesus.

We see in today's gospel that God's motivation toward people is love. God's love is not limited to a few or to one group of people but God's gift is for the whole world. God's love was expressed in the giving of God's most precious gift, Jesus himself! The verse that gets all the attention here is verse 16, "For God so loved the world that he gave his only Son, so that everyone who believes in him may not perish but may have eternal life" (NRSV).

It is illustrative to point out that the Greek word translated "one" or "only," referring to the Son, means, "Only begotten," or "only born-one." This "only born-one" or "Only begotten" gift is to be received not earned by women and men. It is the gift of life and it is given freely for all to receive. When we look at the cross of Calvary, we see death, we see pain, we see suffering, but if we look beyond that, look beyond the physical realities of the cross, what do we see? We see the love of God, we glimpse paradise.

As we look at the old rugged cross, as we see it coming over the horizon this season of Lent, as we begin to hear the sounds of the hammer pounding the nails into the hands of Jesus, as we hear the cry of pain and suffering, we see that beyond all of that, the purpose of the cross was love.

For God so loved the world. God so loved us that God sacrificed the Son, in fact God's only Son to the cross so that we might be set free from the bondage to sin that is such a part of our lives. The cross of Calvary, that old rugged cross, is indeed the emblem of suffering and pain but it is also, and most importantly a symbol of freedom; it was and remains a liberating sign for us because through that cross we are once and for all set free from the bondage of sin, we are allowed to break away from the chains that hold us in darkness, and we are set free to bask in the light of Easter dawn.

In an essay titled "On the Tree," Robert G. Lee, wrote:

> Thus we see that the Cross was substitutionary. On the Cross, where the history of human guilt culminated, He was wounded for our transgressions. On the Cross, where purposes of divine love are made intelligible, He was bruised for our iniquities. As our substitute on the Cross, where the majesty of the law is fulfilled, He bore the penalty of our transgressions and iniquities. "Who his own self bare our sins in his own body on the tree" (1 Peter 2:24 KJV). Only as our substitute could he have borne them. As Abraham offered the ram instead of Isaac his son, so Christ was offered once to bear the sins of man.[1]

I think it is fair to say that there are few if any hymns more powerful and emotional than "The Old Rugged Cross." The text for the hymn comes from John 19:13-22, a text that we will live with on Good Friday. But suffice it to say that this hymn is a timeless message that has penetrated into the very fabric of religious life across all denominational lines.

It was the modern-day prophet, Dr. Martin Luther King Jr., who said, "Calvary is a telescope through which we look into the long vista of eternity, and see the love of God breaking forth into time."

The above quotations and a myriad of others tell us that scripture is quite clear that a person is redeemed by believing and by trusting in Christ. The cross continues to help us see the remarkable way in which God got through to us. One last quote on the subject comes to us from the great Soren Kierkegaard, the French philosopher who declared that "in removing from Christianity its ability to shock, it is altogether destroyed. It becomes a superficial thing, incapable of inflicting deep wounds or of healing them." That is to say that in this instance the cross has the power to shock us into a Christ-centered sanity.

As the words to that famous hymn says:

> On a hill far away stood an old rugged cross,
> The emblem of suffering and shame;
> And I love that old cross where the dearest and best
> For a world of lost sinners was slain.
>
> So I'll cherish the old rugged cross,
> Till my trophies at last I lay down;
> I will cling to the old rugged cross,
> And exchange it some day for a crown.[2]

God did this because God loves us. God did this because God loves those whom God has created. God did this because God could not bear to see us suffer and could not bear to see us separated any longer.

God knew we could not and cannot span the gulf that separates us from the divine presence. And so God built a bridge for us to cross. The material God used in constructing that bridge came from a strong tree and that tree was fashioned into a symbol shaped into the form of a cross. And it was through the cross that God built a channel, an avenue, a roadway for us to once and forever bridge the gap between us.

God, the master builder of creation, designed the bridge for our freedom. Not only that, God designed and built it out of materials that were not indestructible. God did not expect nor ask humankind to build the cross, it was a personal mission that showed forth eternity. And when God was finished, God shared the completed work with all people who would believe that God did the building, all of the building for us!

God shared it with all who would believe that the work was done for them. God used the cross of Calvary, that old rugged cross we sing about, to build a bridge between God and us. As we see the cross coming closer into view, let us look beyond the cross to the see the one who loved us enough to use the cross as the bridge so that we might be granted freedom from sin and released from the bondage to death.

As the hymn says:

> In that old rugged cross, stained with blood so divine,
> A wondrous beauty I see,
> For 'twas on that old cross Jesus suffered and died,
> To pardon and sanctify me.

As the cross comes into sharper focus, we can see the form of one hanging on the cross. We can see the Son of God hanging on the cross, we can see the holes in his hands, the thorns on his head, we can hear his conversations with his Father, and with the people looking at him. We can see a man dying for the rest of humanity; we can see one suffering for the people of the earth. We can see a man feeling forsaken, feeling alone, and feeling the weight of all the sinfulness of creation on his back.

God constructed a way for us to come to God; God doesn't ask us to help bridge the gap, God doesn't ask us to be punished for our own sinfulness but God uses God's only begotten Son for that purpose. As John says, "For God so loved the world that he gave his only Son." Think on that my brothers and sisters in Christ: God gave God's only Son for you!

The last vision for us as we look longingly up at the cross helps us to finally see the truly unbelievable and very personal sacrifice that Jesus offered on our behalf. We can see that he offered himself, he gave of himself, he took the sting of death, the power of death, the pain of death upon himself, so that we won't have to. We know now that because Jesus died and because God raised him on the third day, that we too will be free from the sting and power of death by the victory of the resurrection. Because Jesus offered himself for us we no longer have to fear death, the sting has been removed.

For God so loved the world that he gave his only Son. The love that God has for us allows us to live in a special way, to live God's way. God loved us enough so that we would change and follow him.

Although I have never attended, I am told by a number of church friends that the play that takes place at the Bavarian village of Oberammergau every ten years is an experience never to be forgotten. A cross towers high above the village where the Passion play is presented. No person, I am told, can sit through the eight-hour drama without feeling the accusations of the cross and without finding himself or herself in the crucifixion party. The cross means many things to many people. Whatever theology one embraces, Calvary is where God and humankind meet, and God won!

All God does is love us and it works!

Yes, as the cross, the old rugged cross, comes into sharper view these next few weeks, we can see the great love that God has for us. Through the cross, we can see the great highway God built for us by using the cross and the body and blood of his Son. We can see with even sharpened vision, the one who hung on that cross, we can see the form of Jesus dying for us.

We can see the one who took our place, we can see the one who was willing to change places with us. We can see the one who took our sinful lives and gave us a life of freedom, freedom from sin and freedom from the bondage of death.

As we focus in even closer on the cross, we see that Jesus sacrificed himself, we can see the pain, the punishment, the sting of death he took upon himself so we wouldn't have to. Yes, the cross is coming into sharper focus for us. Let us see the cross as a symbol of love, a symbol of freedom, and a symbol of sacrifice so that we might live as free people who share in the love and goodness of God.

> On a hill far away stood an old rugged cross,
> The emblem of suffering and shame;
> And I love that old cross where the dearest and best
> For a world of lost sinners was slain.
>
> So I'll cherish the old rugged cross,
> Till my trophies at last I lay down;
> I will cling to the old rugged cross,
> And exchange it someday for a crown.

"For God so loved the world that he gave his only Son, that whoever believes in him should not perish but have eternal life." Amen.

---

1. G. Curtis Jones, *1000 Illustrations for Preaching and Teaching* (Nashville: Broadman Press, 1986), 94.
2. "The Old Rugged Cross" in the public domain (Words and Music: George Bennard, 1913).

Life Lived in Glory

Today our Lenten journey takes us to a festival and attending the festival are some Greeks. The mention of Greeks in our text for today is important. They were wanderers of the ancient world and they were seekers of the truth. We can surmise that these Greeks were what was known as "God-fearers" who attended Jewish synagogues and festivals. Their inclusion in this narrative has meaning because it is symbolic of the coming of Gentiles to worship God through Christ.

It is interesting as well that these visiting Greeks approach Philip about seeing Jesus. Why did they feel a need to approach Philip about seeing Jesus? Perhaps it was because Philip had a Greek name. It may be that Philip had some contact with people from the Decapolis area; at any rate they felt comfortable in speaking with him first. It is interesting to note that already in this early stage of the development of the disciples there is a chain of command. Our lesson tells us that, "Philip went and told Andrew; then Andrew and Philip went and told Jesus" (v. 22 NRSV). When you think about it, there were probably any number of people who wanted to speak with Jesus and it was prudent and with an eye to security that the disciples were screening who would be allowed to approach Jesus and who would or would not be allowed to speak with him.

As we enter into the fifth week of our Lenten journey, we can see that throughout this time Jesus has been moving toward Calvary, moving toward the tomb. We see in verse 23 that Jesus is very aware of where he is in terms of the journey when he says, "The hour has come for the Son of Man to be glorified" (v. 23 NRSV).

The great statesman, Winston Churchill, once said, "We make a living by what we get. We make a life by what we give." Jesus is aware that he is going to give the ultimate for the sake of humankind. Our lessons to this point in time all point to Jesus having to forfeit something as he gets closer to the cross.

For most people, death is not something to be discussed casually and for many the subject is strictly off limits. We need to understand that for Jesus death was in a meaningful way his entrance into glory. His willingness to continue on the road to Calvary and to die on that cross signals his absolute obedience to God the Father.

Having traveled this far on our Lenten journey it is critical that we look back and forward in terms of better understanding what this special season is all about.

Lent is that liturgical season of the church's calendar year where we focus on the cost of following Christ. Lent is a time of penance, prayer, preparation for or recollection of our baptism in Christ as we prepare for the celebration of Easter. Observance of Lent is as old as the fourth century. It begins on Ash Wednesday, the fortieth weekday before Easter and it ends at midnight Holy Saturday. Lent is that time of year whereby we turn our attention to the cross. We focus on that which God has given us and we are challenged to go forth and do likewise. Lent is about losing our lives by giving them to Christ and getting eternal life by finding Christ within us. Lent is about loss. It's about losing ourselves in order to find our lives.

Jesus tells us, if we will but listen, that "unless a grain of wheat falls into the earth and dies, it remains just a single grain; but if it dies, it bears much fruit" (v. 24 NRSV). The analogy of a kernel of wheat dying in the ground and producing many seeds teaches that death is necessary for a harvest. The wheat analogy illustrates a general paradoxical principle: Death is the way to life. In Jesus' case, his death led to glory and life not only for himself but also for others.

We can see that in the case of his followers both then and now, the principle remains the same. In order to find the life that Jesus would have us live, we must first "hate" the life we have. That is a difficult idea to handle. Of course Jesus is not talking about hating the things you now love or turning your back on your world. Jesus is saying that there is a giving up that must take place and that in the case of our relationship to him, this giving away has to do with letting go of self-centeredness and letting go of anything that has the potential to come between you and him. In other words anything in your life right now that hinders you from being part of Jesus' life must be rejected. Nothing should be allowed to come between you and your Savior.

The essence of the good news of Jesus Christ is all about loss. An authentic gospel life begins with that recognition. It begins with dying. It begins with a difficult journey to the cross. The true gospel is not just about you coming to Jesus as you are; it's about you being baptized in the death, burial, and resurrection of Jesus Christ. It's about you forfeiting your former life and gaining a new life in Christ. This season is about losing. It's about loss.

This whole idea flies directly into the face of our way of living, at least it is for those of us living in the West. I say that because our modern philosophy of life is a matter of holding on and hanging in. Day in and day out we struggle to hold on to our job, to hold on to our house, to hold on to our family, and to hold on to our money. Jesus' words that "we must lose our lives" create for many of us a conflict of interest. We can't sleep. We are overworked and underpaid. Our minds are constantly going. We are walking on eggshells, looking over our shoulders, and waiting for some disaster to strike.

The truth remains that we are called to follow Jesus as the early disciples followed him. Being a servant of Jesus requires following him even and especially when it is uncomfortable. And we cannot forget that many of his early followers did die! According to tradition, many of the early disciples died as martyrs. Jesus' word was thus a prophecy and also a promise. His true disciples followed him in humiliation and later in honor or glory. "And since we are his children, we will share his treasures — for everything God gives to his Son, Christ, is ours, too. But if we are to share his glory, we must also share his suffering" (Romans 8:17 NLT).

Jesus took the time to be sure that his disciples understood the cost of commitment. He didn't try to hide his emotions. He was in turmoil, "For God made Christ, who never sinned, to be the offering for our sin, so that we could be made right with God through Christ" (2 Corinthians 5:21 NLT). In view of his own emotional response to what was going to happen, it would seem that he had every right to stop his journey and find solace when and where he could. But he did not do that because his birth was for the very purpose of bringing him to this point in time. Jesus willingly expressed his submission to the will of God in the words, "Father, glorify your name" (v. 28a NRSV). And those of us who choose to follow Jesus should stand and embrace his example in spite of the difficulties that being a follower may bring.

Our Lenten journey has clearly shown us that Jesus spent the majority of his life showing his disciples and people in general signs and wonders, yet they still did not believe. He spent his life preaching and teaching about the kingdom of God, about blessedness, righteousness, and truth; yet they still did not believe. He spent his life healing the sick, casting out devils, and raising the dead; yet, they still did not believe.

This always raises the question of what we are to do as his followers. If people had such a hard time believing Jesus while they were quite literally in his presence, what on earth can we do right now to convince people that Jesus was who he said he was?

That is why it is so important to watch what you say and do as you represent yourself as a Christian. What you say and how you present yourself to the wider community are all indications of what you believe, and how what you believe effects how you live. The truth is that these are the things people will look at in how they evaluate who you are and will determine to a large degree how people understand your vocation with Christ.

Watch what you say when confronted with questions about rising gas prices and the decrease in jobs. Watch what you say when people question you about supporting the war. As Christians, we don't support war. We support peace. We pray for those in war. We pray for our soldiers, generals, and leaders. We pray for the opposition and their families but we support peace. Blessed are the peacemakers for they shall inherit the kingdom of God. This is not to say that Christians should remain on the sidelines of life. This is not to say that Christians do or should not complain about certain things in life. But how we say what we have to say and how we voice the things that do not please us is an indicator of how we see life and the living of it.

We are left with the words that Jesus heard thundered from heaven, "Then a voice came from heaven, 'I have glorified it, and I will glorify it again' " (v. 28b NRSV). God is saying as clearly as possible for any who would listen that in Jesus, God has and continues to act. The voice from heaven was a confirmation that Jesus was God's ambassador. That voice confirmed faith in those who were spiritually perceptive but to those who do not believe it was and remains just so much noise. Jesus' journey to the cross was a judgment on

47

the world. We call it the atonement. Evil was atoned for on that day on that hill on that cross. The cross was the means of defeating evil.

When Jesus said the words, "And I, when I am lifted up from the earth, will draw all people to myself" (v. 32 NRSV), refer not to his ascension but to his crucifixion. He knew how he would die, by being "lifted up" on a cross.

Lastly let us remember that the words Jesus spoke above were words that offered great comfort to all who heard them at that time and should indeed do the same for us today. Those words are a promise to the Christian community. To all of you who are struggling with life, for those of you who are struggling with your faith, to those who have tried to explain to a loved one what it is all about and to those who have lost friends because of your faith Jesus says, "I will bring you into myself."

Solomon said for every matter under heaven there is a time and a season; a time to be born and a time to die; a time to plant and a time to pluck up what is planted. This is your season. God has prepared you for this season so that God may be glorified, not you. So that when you come through this period of your life, a time to be born or a time to die, people will be able to look at you and know without question, without a word of doubt, that it was nothing but the grace of God that brought you through.

Lent is a reminder that God would not have brought you to such a time as this, if God did not know that you were prepared for it. Your response and mine, as we go through this season we call life is, "Father, glorify thy name." Be glorified in the heavens. Be glorified in the earth. Be glorified in me, if it be your will. Having said this, we are still faced with the universal question on the lips of anyone who is losing their health; anyone coping with the loss of a loved one, and the question is, "Tell me God, tell me how is it that you are being glorified in my misery? Tell me, preacher, how is God glorified while I see my family struggle and stress?"

The answer is that God is glorified in our willingness to fall before him. God is glorified when we are willing to humble ourselves in God's presence. Like the grain or a seed, we must be willing to fall to the ground and be absorbed by it. A seed is no good and serves no purpose if it is not planted. As long as it remains above ground, where it can be seen, it remains sterile. Just so with all of us; we have no purpose, we make no difference in our community, we have no growth, and there is no fruit of the spirit in our lives if we are not firmly planted in the soil of Jesus Christ. Lent reminds us that without Jesus there is no love, no joy, no peace, no patience, no kindness, no goodness, no faithfulness, no gentleness, and no self-control. To gain our lives in Christ we must be willing to lose ourselves in Christ. We must be willing to lose our identity in order to gain our spirituality.

The good news of the gospel is this, if you are willing to lose your life, to let those worldly concerns die, then you shall gain it. God will be glorified in the life you receive after this temporary existence. You will gain your purpose with the Prince of Peace. Those who seek to save their lives shall lose and those who hate their lives shall gain eternal life. Jesus uses himself as the quintessential premise that even the best of us can still get better. As glorious as Jesus was, he was yet to be glorified. There was still a level of glory for him to ascend. He had yet to be at his best.

I would have thought he was glorified when the heavens opened up and the Holy Spirit descended upon him and God said this is my beloved Son, in whom I'm well pleased but that was not Jesus at his best. I thought maybe he was at his best when Jesus stood on the bow of a boat in the midst of a raging sea, and said, "Peace be still" and the roaring seas became calm, still waters. The winds slowed down to a nice summer breeze. Yet, he was not at his best. Some would have surmised that Jesus was at his best when he raised Lazarus from the dead. But he was still not at his best.

No, Jesus was at his best when he carried an old, rugged cross to a hill called Calvary. Jesus was at his best when he allowed his enemies to nail him to that cross; and yet, pray, "Father, forgive them; for they do not know what they are doing" (Luke 23:34 NRSV). Jesus was at his best when he allowed the cross to mock his name, pierce him in his side, and place a crown of thorns on his head when he could have called down the host of heaven to deliver him from that cross. Jesus was at his best when he called out, "It is finished. Into thy hands, Father, do I commend my Spirit." Jesus was at his best when he allowed them to bury his body in a borrowed tomb. Jesus was at his best when on the third day, he rose, and stood before his disciples and declared, "all authority in heaven and on earth has been given to me" (Matthew 28:18 NRSV).

Listen to me: Your best moment is just ahead. Jesus has gotten the victory, and he has given you power to be his witness to the uttermost parts of the world. And to that we should all say, "Amen."

A View from the Cross

In our text this morning we went to the place where Jesus Christ was crucified. Today we are going to focus on the people gathered around the cross. The view that we find in Mark's gospel is not the view of looking at the cross, but the view that Jesus had from the cross. And the amazing thing about this view from the cross in this present year, is that you can still find the same kinds of personalities that Jesus found when he looked down upon those who had gathered to watch him die.

Simon of Cyrene is the first person mentioned. Can you imagine how Simon felt? Think about it. Simon had come to Jerusalem to celebrate the Passover Feast. He had traveled all the way from Cyrene, an important city on the coast of North Africa that had a large Jewish colony. Simon was either an immigrant living in Jerusalem or more likely, one of the many thousands of pilgrims coming for the Passover festival. Mark is the only gospel that tells us that Simon had sons, Alexander and Rufus, suggesting that they were disciples known to his readers in Rome. Paul wrote in Romans, "Greet Rufus, whom the Lord picked out to be his very own; and also his dear mother, who has been a mother to me" (Romans 16:13 NLT).

You have to admit that you would not have wanted to be in Simon's place. He had come to the Passover festival and carrying a cross was certainly not part of his plans for the day. I'm sure he was angry about this interruption. Undoubtedly his attitude was one of unwilling involvement. Carrying a cross to the hill where criminals were crucified was anything but pleasant.

As we gather on this special day I think it is fair to say that there are many people who are resentful that God would dare change their plans, especially if it meant picking up a cross and carrying it for Jesus. We don't want things to happen to us by surprises that don't fit into our routine. Most of us resent it when some circumstance over which we have no control suddenly changes our plans, especially if it involves pain and suffering. But that is reality and it is one that all of us have to live with from time to time.

Next, the Roman soldiers took Jesus to the place outside but close to the city gates so all who passed by could witness those who were being crucified. The hill where they sank the crosses into the stony earth was commonly called Golgotha, a Greek transliteration of an Aramaic word meaning, the *place of the skull*. Golgotha was a rounded, rocky outcropping that some said resembled the shape of a human skull.

Gathered around the foot of the cross were the soldiers who had crucified Jesus. These rough Roman soldiers had crucified many people. They undoubtedly had much experience in crucifixion, because when they had finished their work and Jesus was hanging from the cross, these soldiers got out a pair of dice and started a craps game at the foot of the cross.

It seems strange to us that anyone could contemplate the dying of Jesus and carry on in such a way, but here were men who were far more interested in making a buck than they were in the suffering of Jesus or the others there crucified with him.

You know before we become a bit too judgmental we have to at least entertain the notion that we too, in this present time have many people who are not at all concerned about the meaning of the death of Christ. Far too often our whole concern is focused on making a fast buck, just like those soldiers. These soldiers stand forever as examples of those callous individuals who have no interest in the great story of the cross, who shrug their shoulders with indifference to anybody who tries to call their attention to what was really happening on that horrible hill.

As we continue our journey into the Passion of our Lord we are joined by the robbers. Here are two men who had been arrested because of their acts of terror and violence. In today's world they may have been called terrorists because they were professional revolutionaries. They were angry young men, committed to the philosophy of getting what you can any way that you can get it, regardless of who gets hurt in the process. These two looked upon Jesus as the same kind of man. They hated him because he was of no more help to them than they could be to him. However, at sometime during the time they hung next to Jesus dying, one of these men had a change of heart. One of these robbers asked Jesus to remember him when he came into his kingdom (Luke 23:40-43).

The fact remains that there are still many today that even at the point of death are filled with enough hate and indifference to mock Jesus. There are still many today who question the power of Christ. There are still many today who seem to think that Jesus was no different than we are, but there are also many who see the need for the Savior and they are next in our story.

In verse 15:29, Mark tells us that there were certain passersby who came by the cross as Jesus was suspended on it. These were just bystanders, but when they saw Jesus, they remembered that he was the one who had made these great claims, and they said, "Look, they've caught you, haven't they? You've gone too far. You were doing fine teaching the people, but then you began making these ridiculous claims that you could destroy the temple and raise it up again. You got what you had coming." They were enjoying the verbal abuse that they put upon Jesus.

I would like to say that things have changed dramatically since that time, but that would not be truthful. Today, in the year 2012 there are many that claim to be followers of Jesus, but when someone says something like, "Jesus is the way and the truth and the life," they back off because they are worried about offending someone who does not feel that way. It is true that we live in a pluralistic society, but that does not change who we are as Christians or at least it should not change that truth. Some people would rather spend their time arguing about whether God made the world in an actual week, or they are worried about the virgin birth or the way to salvation, rather than owning their faith and living out that faith at the foot of the cross.

The leading priests and teachers of religious law also mocked Jesus at the foot of the cross. "He saved others," they scoffed, "but he can't save himself! Let this Messiah, this king of Israel, come down from the cross so we can see it and believe him!" Even the two criminals who were being crucified with Jesus ridiculed him (Mark 15:31-32 NLT). It is important to see these priests had been very frightened of Jesus before, but now they were very arrogant. Before, they were threatened by him but now what could he do to them? They screamed out words to Jesus to come down off the cross and then they would believe. They wanted Jesus to abandon the cross. You know, you can just see these guys mocking Jesus. There is a mean streak that runs through most people that usually goes unseen. It is a mean-spirited streak that most people keep in check but occasionally it gets out and these leading priests have let loose their inner hatred and anger.

I would like to think that we are better today than they were then. But the truth of the matter is that there are still religious leaders today who would like us to abandon the cross. It is too gory and bloody they say. However, we must realize that the cross is at the very center of the good news of Jesus Christ. Whether they like it or not, that gory and bloody cross Jesus Christ hung upon is the only way to say out loud that on that cross Jesus paid it all! It is in vogue today to build new sanctuaries without the presence of a cross because too many in the world feel the cross is just too hard to view. Well, it was meant to be hard to view.

Mark tells us that some of the bystanders who were at the cross found it a bit confusing because they thought that Jesus was calling out to Elijah. One of them ran and filled a sponge with sour wine, holding it up to him on a stick so he could drink. Leave him alone. "Let's see whether Elijah will come and take him down!" he said (Mark 15: 35-36 NLT). We do not know the names of these people and at first glance, it looks like this man is concerned about Jesus. He runs to get vinegar, which would deaden the pain of suffering and he filled a sponge with it and put it to Jesus' lips. It looks like he is trying to help, but if you look at this account carefully that is not his motive at all. His motive is to see if something exciting will happen. He is not moved by compassion but by curiosity. Remember that Jesus is still awake and he can see what is going on. The view from the cross is never an easy one.

Today things are much the same. I read an account not that long ago about a man who was threatening to jump off the George Washington Bridge. At first several cars pulled over pleading with the man to step back from the railing and not to jump. But the longer the ordeal played out, the stranger the response of people became, until finally a few people just yelled for the guy to go ahead and jump! Who would say such a thing? People who are seeking thrills, people who would stand under the cross and mock Jesus, that's who. We have people that come to our churches not to seek the Savior but to seek a thrill and when they don't find that thrill, they don't come back. As I said above, the view from the cross may turn you off, it is not pretty, but if you wait and if you pay attention you just may end up being saved from jumping off that bridge in your life whatever it may be.

It is at this place in our reading that Jesus dies. Mark still has three more accounts about the people who gathered around the cross but these are people of a different character. These are people who love Jesus, they see what is going on, although they do not necessarily understand what is happening, they know it is life changing.

These are people that you may not have thought would be filled with compassion but there they were. One person you would not have guessed to be a player in this story is the centurion who was in charge of the crucifixion. He had witnessed many such crucifixions in life and he was probably a pagan. He probably believed in many gods. Yet the cross brought to him awareness that what he was watching was no joke. There had been a terrible mistake made. This centurion sees that Jesus was indeed the Son of God, but there is no understanding that there may be help for him in the process. After all, what good could possibly come from a crucifixion?

This wonderful season brings with it the chance that some Christians may still not have a clear view of the cross. I do think that it is still the case today that many people understand God is at work in the death of Jesus. They understand that Jesus was more than just a man but it never gets any further. They are impressed by the cross and impressed by the character of Jesus but it never becomes personalized and they never enter into the value of that death.

There is another scene that is critically important for us today. It is a scene that is played out in most churches every week. We might simply yell out, "Where are the men?" It is a legitimate question, because there were plenty of women around the cross but where were the men? These women were not gathering around the cross in hope but in hopelessness. This is a picture of hopeless commitment. These women were there because of their love for Jesus. But where were the men? There is no need to try to answer that question today but you have to admit it is a good one!

There are many today who believe in God. They believe in the record of the scripture. They believe that God is there and that God works until it comes to that moment of a crisis in their own life. Then their hope is gone. They really have no hope that God actually will act in the hour of despair. While their love remains, their hope and faith are gone. Their faith is strong as long as everything goes well but when the bottom drops out, they still love but their faith is gone.

It is into this situation that Joseph of Arimathea makes an appearance. Mark relates one final scene in verses 42-47.

> This all happened on Friday, the day of preparation, the day before the sabbath. As evening approached, an honored member of the high council, Joseph from Arimathea (who was waiting for the kingdom of God to come), gathered his courage and went to Pilate to ask for Jesus' body. Pilate couldn't believe that Jesus was already dead, so he called for the Roman military officer in charge and asked him. The officer confirmed the fact, and Pilate told Joseph he could have the body. Joseph bought a long sheet of linen cloth, and taking Jesus' body down from the cross, he wrapped it in the cloth and laid it in a tomb that had been carved out of the rock. Then he rolled a stone in front of the entrance. Mary Magdalene and Mary the mother of Joseph saw where Jesus' body was laid.
>
> — Mark 15:42-47 NLT

Here is Joseph of Arimathea and where has he been before this? Well, that is a good question. Would it be fair to call him a stealth disciple, looking for the kingdom of God? Obviously Joseph was in some way attracted to Jesus but he was frightened to show himself or to be vocal about it.

We have no record of him ever saying anything before this moment but here he is.

We must not rush to a judgment on him for his silence. His silence is no different than our own. Too often we remain silent about our faith until some moment of crisis forces us to step and speak out. The Lenten season and this Holy Week should be an eye opener to us all that the cross is not a silent sentinel. The cross speaks out to us who are standing around waiting to see what is going to happen. The death of Jesus opened Joseph's eyes and it should do the same for us all. Open your eyes and see; open your eyes, open your hearts and see what Jesus saw from that cruel instrument of torture. He saw people just like us. Look around you, really look and you will see the same people Jesus saw! Joseph found his courage under the cross, where will you find yours? Amen.

Maundy Thursday
John 13:1-17, 31b-35

The Perfect Example to Follow

As is often the case, John's gospel reports more of the contents of Jesus' instructions to his disciples than do the other three gospels. There are always detractors but it seems that one of the reasons for this was the fact that John is an eyewitness to all that he writes about.

As we have seen during our Lenten journey, Jesus' own journey was headed for the cross and finally the empty tomb. Here in John 13, we can surmise that Jesus' death and resurrection were now imminent. He had come a long way and he knew that he had come in obedience to his Father's will. We can see that in his obedience he was also acting in love for all of humankind. It seems quite clear that he had a special kind of love for those who had chosen to follow him and had stayed with him through all of the turbulence that accompanied them all in getting to this point.

During the American Revolution a man in civilian clothes rode past a group of soldiers repairing a small defensive barrier. Their leader was shouting instructions but making no attempt to help them. Asked why by the rider, he retorted with great dignity, "Sir, I am a corporal!" The stranger apologized, dismounted, and proceeded to help the exhausted soldiers. The job done, he turned to the corporal and said, "Mr. Corporal, next time you have a job like this and not enough men to do it, go to your commander-in-chief, and I will come and help you again." It was none other than George Washington.[1] Today we're going to talk about the example set by Jesus for all of us to follow. His words and actions are words and actions that all of us would do well to live by.

Let us recall that as we approach the evening meal outlined in our reading, Judas has already undertaken his hateful act of cowardice. It is remarkable to watch as Jesus voluntarily took the place of a servant, washing the feet of his disciples, even in the midst of betrayal.

We should remember that foot washing was not a foreign action at all. In point of fact, it was a needed service for those who traveled the dusty and dirty roads where Jesus and his followers traveled daily. No one wore socks because there were none! It was an act of honor on behalf of a host to wash a guest's feet, and it was a sign of dishonor not to do so. It was not uncommon for wives to wash their husband's feet and for children to do the same for their parents.

It is only natural that Peter, wanting Jesus to be above the common everyday things that people lived with, was not at all happy with Jesus becoming the servant of anyone, especially the disciples. Peter just did not feel that Jesus should act like a servant but especially not as Peter's servant. Unthinkable! Peter, as usual, speaks what he feels without giving it a whole lot of thought. Jesus tells him to his face that he has to wash Peter's feet. Peter, however, remains skeptical and really is not in line with Jesus' thought process.

Continuing to miss the point, Peter asked Jesus to also wash his hands and his head and his feet. Jesus replied that a person who is already clean doesn't need his whole body washed again but their feet would still need attention. Then Jesus goes on to say that not everyone who was with him was clean. He was, of course, referring to Judas.

On this Maundy Thursday let me ask you all a question. What would you do if you knew you would die a violent death in about twelve hours? Would you want to be alone in prayer? Would you record some final thoughts? Would you spend time with those you loved? What would you want to emphasize? Would you share recipes or gardening tips or would you focus on what's most important in your life?

As was said earlier, the Bible tells us that Jesus knew the time had come for him to leave this world and he took off his cloak, put a towel around his waist, and washed the dirty feet of his disciples. Who's going to waste time on that when the end is so near? Jesus. Why? Because he wanted to show them how important it is to humbly serve one another and,

> Don't be selfish; don't live to make a good impression on others. Be humble, thinking of others as better than yourself. Don't think only about your own affairs, but be interested in others, too, and what they are doing. Your attitude should be the same that Christ Jesus had. Though he was God, he did not demand and cling to his rights as God. He made himself nothing; he took the humble position of a slave and appeared in human form. And in human form he obediently humbled himself even further by dying a criminal's death on a cross.
> — Philippians 2:3-8 NLT

Mother Teresa visited Phoenix in 1989 to open a home for the poor. During that brief visit, she was interviewed by KTAR, the largest radio station in town. In a private moment, the announcer asked Mother Teresa if there was anything he could do for her. He was expecting her to request a contribution or media attention to help to raise money for the new home for the needy in Phoenix. Instead, she replied, "Yes, there is. Find somebody nobody else loves, and love them."

Jesus showed by his own actions that serving others, demonstrating our love in tangible ways, is of critical importance. Jesus considered it a priority and so should we.

The scripture says that not just in spite of but because he understood who he was, Jesus washed the disciples' feet. It takes an understanding of our identity to be able to humble ourselves. The world tells us that we need to make ourselves look good in front of others that we need to lift ourselves up and demonstrate how important we are. I am not about to say the Bible has an answer for everything because technically speaking it does not. What it does tell us on a human level is, "But those who exalt themselves will be humbled, and those who humble themselves will be exalted" (Matthew 23:12 NLT).

It is like the corporal who couldn't humble himself and was humbled by the commander-in-chief. If we don't understand who we are in Jesus, we will be unwilling to humble ourselves until the Lord himself humbles us.

The late Dave Thomas, founder of Wendy's hamburger chain, was known for his humble service within the multibillion dollar empire he founded. When asked what made him so successful, he replied, "my MBA." But he didn't mean a graduate degree in business education he meant "a mop-and-bucket attitude." In other words, no task was too insignificant for him to tackle; he simply jumped in and got the job done.

If anyone didn't have to humble himself to wash the feet of a bunch of fishermen, it was Jesus. Because he knew he was Lord of the universe and because he was not worried about his self-image he was able to show his love in humble service. He took up the towel and basin and stooped to serve. What an example for us all.

On this special night it is also important that we try to discover our need to be in Jesus' presence and the additional need of being served by Jesus himself. Sometimes that is a hard idea to come to grips with. Look again at the exchange between Peter and Jesus,

> When he came to Simon Peter, Peter said to him, "Lord, why are you going to wash my feet?" Jesus replied, "You don't understand now why I am doing it; someday you will." "No," Peter protested, "you

will never wash my feet!" Jesus replied, "But if I don't wash you, you won't belong to me." Simon Peter exclaimed, "Then wash my hands and head as well, Lord, not just my feet!"

— John 13:6-9 (NLT)

You see when Jesus himself makes it clear that being the one served by Jesus is one of the conditions for having a relationship with him, Peter has a change of heart. I think there is clearly some symbolism here. Jesus is saying not just that Peter must let him wash his feet, but the reference is to the more thorough washing that Jesus will perform the next day when his blood is shed for Peter's sin and for ours.

I hope that we will all be able to identify with Peter here. The truth is that our pride often gets in the way of our living the life Jesus wants us to live. We all want other people to think well of us and there is nothing wrong with that, unless it gets in the way of our walk with the Lord. By our own effort we each will only be able to go so far. The message to Peter and to us all is that unless we let Jesus wash us, we have no part with him. Unless we recognize the mistake of our pride — the mistake that says, "I'm good enough on my own," then we make no room for Jesus and we will never come to the point of being able to say along with Peter, "Then wash my hands and head as well, Lord, not just my feet!" With any luck we will come to our senses enough to recognize how wonderful it will be for each of us to become servants in the service of Jesus.

Jesus has shown us by word and deed that you cannot call yourself a Christian if you are unwilling to serve in humility. That doesn't mean we don't have individual gifts and places of service, sometimes very public ones, roles of leadership, but each of us should be willing to humble ourselves, to demonstrate our love for those we serve. Remember how our first president got off his horse to help that soldier? Isn't that as good an example as we need?

You see foot washing isn't about foot washing, it's about serving others at personal sacrifice, humbling ourselves when we don't have to because we don't have to. It's somebody watching the children of a neighbor who has good reasons for needing to get out of the house. It is people showing up at another's door with hot soup on a cold night knowing that the folk in need have lost power; it is about clearing someone's driveway of snow because you know they are not healthy enough to do it themselves. It's listening to a neighbor who needs to talk when you don't have time to listen. It's giving ourselves when we don't have to. It is walking and talking with Jesus on the road we call life. It is about sharing a meal as darkness approaches. It is about washing our lives in the promises of our Savior and being diligent in waiting with him as the world becomes a dark place. It is about standing at the foot of a cross and in faithfulness standing by an empty tomb as the darkness is lifted and life becomes hopeful once again. Amen.

---

1. *Today in the Word*, March 6, 1991.

From the Courtroom to the Cross — A King's Journey

John records more details of the crucial events of the trial and crucifixion of Jesus than any other of the gospels. Many believe that John was able to report in such detail because he was present to witness what he was writing about. Even more importantly, it is because John had a more intimate relationship with Jesus. It seems fair to speculate that the knowledge he gained from that relationship can be found in the intricate way in which this gospel account is written.

The action in John's gospel moves quickly from one scene to another. We go from the Jewish court to the Roman tribunal in quick succession. Once again we see that the way in which someone remembers and records events can have far-reaching consequences on the way in which the message is received. We can almost feel the stress level as John describes Peter pulling out his sword and waving it around, striking the high priest's slave and cutting off his ear. We can also feel the deception in Judas' kiss. John's gospel takes us by the hand and we are invited to walk and eavesdrop as John is jostled by the crowd while trying to follow Jesus to the house of the high priest. One can only imagine the pain and confusion that John felt as Jesus was escorted into the residence of the Roman governor. Events were moving quickly, way too fast for John or the other disciples to grasp what was about to happen.

Only John explains the reasons Jesus was delivered to the Romans as he was. Jewish executions were normally done by stoning. The Roman method of execution was by crucifixion. History tells us that it was necessary Jesus be dealt with the way he was for three reasons. First was to fulfill prophecy specifically that

> These things happened in fulfillment of the scriptures that say, "Not one of his bones will be broken," and "They will look on him whom they pierced."
> — John 19:36-37 NLT

> Second, it was necessary to include both Jews and Gentiles in what was about to happen, "But you followed God's prearranged plan. With the help of lawless Gentiles, you nailed him to the cross and murdered him."
> — Acts 2:23 NLT

> And finally, by crucifixion, "And as Moses lifted up the bronze snake on a pole in the wilderness, so I, the Son of Man, must be lifted up on a pole."
> — John 3:14 NLT

We know that Pilate had private time to talk with Jesus. Pilate knew that it was not normal for the Jewish authorities to turn over one of their own, especially to the hated Romans who occupied their tiny country. Luke's gospel tells us Jesus was accused of subverting the nation, being opposed to payment of taxes, and that Jesus claimed to be a king.

The charge that Jesus claimed to be a king was the one that carried the most legal weight with the authorities. This is the kind of claim that dictators take seriously. One need only see our own recent world political turmoil to see how much power that kind of statement can have. So it is not surprising that Pilate asks Jesus straight out,

> "Are you the king of the Jews?" Jesus replied, "Is this your own question, or did others tell you about me?" "Am I a Jew?" Pilate asked. "Your own people and their leading priests brought you here. Why? What

have you done?" Then Jesus answered, "I am not an earthly king. If I were, my followers would have fought when I was arrested by the Jewish leaders. But my kingdom is not of this world." Pilate replied, "You are a king then?" "You say that I am a king, and you are right," Jesus said. "I was born for that purpose. And I came to bring truth to the world. All who love the truth recognize that what I say is true." "What is truth?" Pilate asked. Then he went out again to the people and told them, "He is not guilty of any crime."
— John 18:33-38 NLT

It is very instructive that Jesus said, "I am not an earthly king." This statement added fuel to the fire and served as the catalyst that pushed Pilate to take action against Jesus. He just could not ignore that claim. What is this Jesus talking about? He seemed a nice enough guy, why was he doing this? The kingdom he spoke of isn't even in a geographic location that can be identified on any map.

All of this leads to one of the great conundrums in scripture. There is little doubt that Jesus refers to his kingdom in these verses. But nowhere in all of the biblical record can we ever find Jesus himself stating, "I am a king." As often as we think of him as the king, calling him our king is our doing, not his. In the book of Revelation, John will even go so far as to call him the "King of kings," and the "Lord of lords," but Jesus never makes this claim of himself. This fact is followed by another where Jesus shows us by his own actions that he has come to bear witness to the truth, but what that truth is will have to wait for an unveiling at the cross and an introduction to the world at an empty tomb.

It is important to keep in mind the Jewish people have a long history of being a conquered people. That history goes back to the Egyptians, then the conquest of northern Judea by the Assyrians; the defeat of Southern Israel by Babylon; then the Greeks under Alexander the Great. Here they are under the Roman emperor. At this specific time in history, when

Jesus' ministry is unfolding, the man who holds the office of the Jewish king, Herod, is only a figurehead appointed by Rome. It is Caesar who calls all the shots. Into this political mess walks Jesus, the King of all kings and Lord over all other lords. Again, put it all into context, Jesus makes no demands for allegiance. There is no conquest. There is no force by arms. Jesus doesn't demand anything but instead he asks those who would follow him who they think he is. The response to that question is always interesting because it adds to the mystery. I say that because his own closest friends, the disciples, did not know who he was. Oh, to be sure they had hopes and dreams about who he was, or at the very least, who they wanted him to be. However, they would not figure it all out until after Easter. But, let's step back as it is way too easy to get ahead of ourselves.

There is so much going on in the verses for this day. It is tempting to move too quickly so we can get to Easter. The truth is that because of the history of Jesus' own people, and because that history is filled with such violence, a new paradigm is needed and Jesus is going to provide that new way of living and looking at life. Jesus in his time of trial shows peace in a way that defined his ministry and therefore our own religious existence to this day. Jesus knew that to live by violence only brought about more of the same. Sadly, we have not learned to handle violence much better than the Romans when they dealt with Jesus. Jesus shows how to handle evil. It is interesting to take note of the fact that the people with the weapons, the Romans, did not ever unsheathe their weapons when Jesus was on his way to the cross. Why? Because they were not needed! Jesus' aggressive love ruled the day, even in the midst of such cruel treatment. When you read the account of Pilate and Jesus you can see that it produces some moving scenes. We see Pilate — a man who wanted to do right — but did not have the courage or character to do what was right.

The Jewish leaders who brought Jesus to Pilate asked for the death penalty with no trial at all. Pilate refused this request. Next, Jesus was accused of a political crime. The whole king controversy we have discussed already.

The brutal scourging prior to any verdict was not what should have been expected of Pilate at this stage in the proceedings. In all probability he did it to ease the pressure he must have been feeling from those who had brought Jesus to be killed. There was still no guilt to be found in Jesus.

The accusations were not over just yet. The next charge was religious in nature. It led to one of the many trips that the bewildered Roman ruler made from outside where the Jews gathered to inside where Jesus was waiting patiently for whatever it was that was going to happen next.

Here Pilate gets a little shaky. Pilate could not be moved to do anything until he was hit at his weakest point. He suddenly turned frightened when mention was made of Caesar: Then Pilate tried to release him, but the Jewish leaders told him, "If you release this man, you are not a friend of Caesar. Anyone who declares himself a king is a rebel against Caesar" (John 19:12 NLT). That was the kind of threat that Pilate could not ignore. Pilate had a bad history with the local people and they had already complained about him to Caesar. Pilate was just plain afraid of another charge, so he gave in and: "Then Pilate gave Jesus to them to be crucified. So they took Jesus and led him away" (John 19:16 NLT).

It seems almost prophetic that the inscription appearing over the head of Jesus as he hung on the cross read, "Jesus of Nazareth, the King of the Jews." The place where Jesus was crucified was near the city; and the sign was written in Hebrew, Latin, and Greek, so that many people could read it (John 19:19-20 NLT). Hebrew was the language of the people. Latin was the language of those in power. And Greek was the common language of the world at that time. Clearly Pilate at least wanted the whole world to know what had happened and that he held the power of life and death and he alone could order Jesus to be crucified. Having said that, the same message must have been a mixed message to the Jewish leaders, "King of the Jews!"

On this Good Friday we all need to come to an understanding that it is not enough to stand frightened and confused under the cross. Hoping that what has happened did not happen will not make it all go away. The cross is real, the nails that pierced his hands and feet are real, the crown of thorns is real. Up until this critical point in our journey to the cross, we have been walking with the disciples. But today we must stand aside and internalize the truth that what we are witnessing is not simply a tragedy for the followers of our Lord. The crucifixion was an act of love! It is a radical way of thinking about life and death and about relationships. It is so hard to put this into words this day. What has happened on the cross is a deliberate act of loving sacrifice for us all. We can say no to a tragedy and even deny it ever happening; but not so with a sacrifice. A sacrifice must be accepted.

John said that Jesus was "the lamb of God." When the lamb was offered as a sacrifice for sin it was not for the lamb's sin, it was for ours! Without accepting this reality, Easter has no meaning.

Those of us in ministry understand the truth that the church only works when it is accepted that it cannot function without volunteers. The thing that is quite different about the church and other organizations is that the volunteers in the church follow a king. In a variety of ways our reading for today, indeed our gospel readings for this entire Lent and Easter season, tell us that Jesus is not looking for volunteers. Jesus is looking for subjects. He's looking for servants who will give their all for him. "If anyone wants to follow me, they must take up their cross daily and follow me" (Luke 9:23 NLT). Take a moment and conjure up an image of the king and his subjects. Think of some movie that has the Knights of the Round Table gathered around their king. There was always a scene where the knights bowed before their king and vowed allegiance. Their life, their wealth, their hearts were forevermore the king's to command. Just a movie, I know, but still it is an image that is worthy of our Lord. The King of kings is seeking those who will give their all for him. Those who will seek his will even before their own. And isn't this what we pray for every Sunday when we pray, "Thy kingdom come, yhy will be done, On earth, as it is in heaven."

In the mid-seventeenth century, Oliver Cromwell sent his secretary to the continent on some important state business. One night during his travels he found he was unable to sleep. According to an old custom a servant slept in his room and that evening the servant was sleeping soundly. In the middle of the night the secretary woke the man up to tell the servant that he could not rest because "I am so afraid something will go wrong with the diplomatic mission," "Master," said the valet, "may I ask a question or two?" "Of course" "Did God rule the world before we were born?" "Most assuredly he did." "And will he rule it after we are dead?" "Certainly he will." "Then, master, why not let him rule the present, too?" The servant's reply so stirred the secretary's faith he found a deep sense of peace, and in a few minutes both he and the servant were sound asleep.

Christians claim that Jesus is the Christ, the King of kings, the Lord of lords. Yet, how often we forget just what that means for our lives. On this Good Friday let me remind you that Jesus Christ is Lord. He was king before Pilate. He was lord of Cromwell's secretary. He will be king at the end of time. He will be Lord when he comes again and he is our Lord and king today. Amen.

Easter Day
John 20:1-18

The Gardens of Life

I look forward to spring and I guess that we all do especially when we have had a hard winter. You know many of us around here say that as soon as spring training starts for our favorite baseball team, no matter how much snow falls, we know it will not last and that as soon as it melts, someone somewhere will be yelling, "Play ball!" It is a rite of passage. It is a good thing!

The same can be said for putting in your garden. I know many of you are very particular about when you start planting and what gets planted when. First you have to till the soil and then you spread the fertilizer and only then will you decide what will go in each row. It is a labor of love that has the unique ability to put you into the position of actually feeling as if you and the earth share a common characteristic. The act of digging and spreading the soil and generally getting your hands dirty makes you feel creative. It makes you feel like God must have felt when he put all of this in place just for you!

I think it is fair to say that gardening is an activity that has the potential to put you closer to God than most anything else you do. I know that those who spend a lot of time outdoors doing other activities feel the same way. Being close to God is sometimes as easy as digging a hole!

Easter takes us on a journey that puts us in touch with the earth. It does so by bringing us into an awareness of the gardens of our life. Not just the ones we physically plant, but those gardens that have served to bring us all closer to God, and therefore closer to our risen Savior. Today I want to invite you to visit some of the Bible's favorite gardening spots. If we pay attention we just may see that the gardener, the one who tills and plants and harvests the crop is the same one who created the seed that is us, planted that seed and nurtured it into full growth. Indeed we just may discover that the reason God bothers with the garden at all is that God loves all who have been planted and wants eternally to care for each and every one of us.

Very likely the first garden that most of us ever heard of is the Garden of Eden. Most of us heard about that garden in our Sunday school classes when we were children. We probably didn't think too much about the particulars, because when you're a child, you really don't care. But as you get older you begin to recognize that the garden described in Genesis is pretty much perfect. The actual account in Genesis says:

> Then the Lord God planted a garden in Eden, in the east, and there he placed the man he had created. And the Lord God planted all sorts of trees in the garden — beautiful trees that produced delicious fruit. At the center of the garden he placed the tree of life and the tree of the knowledge of good and evil. A river flowed from the land of Eden, watering the garden and then dividing into four branches. One of these branches is the Pishon, which flows around the entire land of Havilah, where gold is found. The gold of that land is exceptionally pure; aromatic resin and onyx stone are also found there. The second branch is the Gihon, which flows around the entire land of Cush. The third branch is the Tigris, which flows to the east of Asshur. The fourth branch is the Euphrates. The Lord God placed the man in the Garden of Eden to tend and care for it.
>
> — Genesis 2:8-15 NLT

The Garden of Eden was created as an act of love. But more than that, it was created in a way that allowed interaction between God and humankind. In this garden God created the opportunity for humankind to return love to God and be in a pure relationship with God. The tree of knowledge of good and evil was not a specific type of tree, like a pine tree or an evergreen. Rather the tree represented a way for humankind to show their love to God by not eating the fruit of its branches. The tree created for us the opportunity to choose to follow God or not. We shouldn't concern ourselves with what kind of tree or fruit — in the end all of that is irrelevant.

Genesis goes to great lengths to describe this garden and if the kind of tree and fruit were important, it would have been described in detail. If eating the fruit was a sin then the name of the fruit would be made clear so that we could avoid it. Although it is good for storybooks and pictures, the fruit is secondary to our willfully deciding to separate ourselves from the gardener. Truthfully look what we have managed to do with the concept of sin. One of the single most popular destinations in the United States advertises itself as "Sin City" and tells us that whatever we do in Vegas, stays in Vegas. As if we do not know the difference between good and evil!

You have to admit that naming the tree "the tree of knowledge of good and evil" is a little suspect. But the name really derives from what took place at the tree. The tree got its name when humankind partook of that fruit and discovered something not known before. What was discovered was betrayal, disappointment, and sorrow. What was discovered was the difference between good and evil that was not known before. Our eyes were opened to sin. God then had to send us out of the garden to make sure that we did not take of the tree of life and live forever in sin.

The Garden of Eden shows us that God is the creator, and that God is both personal and eternal. It shows us that God wants to be involved in our lives. The Garden of Eden shows us that the world as we know it did not happen by accident. It shows us that life could not be lived without relationships and without our understanding that we are accountable not only to one another but especially to the one who created us in the first place.

We define ourselves. We regulate ourselves. The Garden of Eden shows us that we do not do a very good job of either defining or regulating what and who we are. All you need to do to see how inept we are at caring for ourselves is to notice the number of laws the free world must enact in order to keep us from killing ourselves and destroying the garden. That is why God does not leave us in charge of the garden, at least not completely. But God does speak to us in creation and tells us that in order to care properly for the garden, we must learn to love God and to love one another. Seems so simple; yet it often takes a lifetime to accomplish.

When God spoke to us in the garden and we did not listen, humanism was born and we mistakenly thought that we and not God contained the source of all meaning. Sadly far too many people still think that way.

One other thing was planted in this garden that we ignore at our own peril. Just as the seed of humanism and sin were planted in this garden, so too was the seed of salvation. The story of redemption begins in the same garden that is so easily defined as the place where sin dominates.

In Matthew 4, we have the story of when Jesus after having been baptized was led out into the desert to be tempted by Satan. For forty days and nights God allowed Jesus to be weakened due to fasting. But it was only when Jesus had been weakened that Satan came and tempted Jesus three times. Satan was tempting Jesus to act in a supernatural way, and Satan knew that if Jesus claimed his power in this way he would be giving into temptation and he would be no better than any other person walking around in the desert garden. The garden in the desert is a garden of deception. It is a garden of misunderstanding and deceit. It is a garden that too many of us know only too well. In the garden of the desert Satan tried to deceive Jesus to use his divine powers and thus rob Jesus of the chance to complete God's business. To fall to Satan would make Jesus only human and eliminate the cross forever.

A quick look back at Hebrew scripture tells us when God sent the plagues on Egypt, those plagues had been designed to show Pharaoh and the others that God alone had power over the objects they worshiped and there was no other like God, period! The temptation in the desert is still with us today. The temptation is to have religion without God, or more to the point to have a religion where we are God! In the desert garden we learn that we cannot pick and choose what God will be like based on the way we want God to be. Jesus was victorious in the garden of the desert and because of that victory over temptation the seed of redemption came more fully into bloom and the journey to the cross would continue. The seed that had been planted in Eden, the seed that was refined and tested in the desert, was preparing to come into full bloom at a rocky and desolate place called Golgotha.

On this special day we really need to remember the temptation to go our own way is forever with us. In Eden, humankind gave in to that testing and fell. In the desert Jesus remained strong but nowhere in scripture is it more clearly evidenced that Jesus throughout his life had the temptation to go his own way, than at the Garden of Gethsemane.

It is in Gethsemane where we see Jesus at his most human state. We have all been there at some point in our own lives. There are times when we all look for a way out, a way to escape from our lives if only for a moment.

You will remember that Jesus was tormented with what was about to happen to him and he went on a little farther and fell face down on the ground, praying, "My Father! If it is possible, let this cup of suffering be taken away from me. Yet I want your will, not mine" (Matthew 26:39 NLT).

If ever there was a prayer of desperation and intensity, this is it.

This Garden of Gethsemane becomes a symbol of the struggle of the journey of faith that all Christians must take. If Jesus struggled so intently over this, how can we expect to live our lives without something similar happening to us? We all face times of abandonment and isolation. We all face times of uncertainty mingled with hope. That is what it is to be human and to be part of the community.

Jesus found himself yielding to God just as all of us must do. As a result of Jesus' giving in or yielding to God, he was nailed to a cross! Until he bowed down before his creator in obedience, there could be no crucifixion. Once he asked for that cup to be removed and then saw that he was asking only for himself, he gave himself over fully to God and left the Garden of Gethsemane prepared for the cross and the tomb that awaited him.

Someone once said that the Garden of Gethsemane gives us a look into the only time in biblical history that Jesus and God have a disagreement. Jesus' prayer in the garden is heartfelt but it is also painful. The end result was Jesus surrendering himself fully to God and that is good news for us all!

That Garden of Gethsemane is the place where humanity with all its flaws comes to agree with divinity. In a very real way you agree to be crucified. You capitulate even when everything in you says to turn back. While there, you might be comforted in remembering this: You will never be closer to the human side of your Lord than in Gethsemane.

The Garden of Gethsemane presents us with a time that two wills are tested to the extreme and come out of that testing in total agreement. For a moment those two wills disagreed. Once that disagreement was settled, their wills became eternally one. The center of that disagreement was a bloody cross; the disagreement was settled in a garden.

It is no wonder then that Paul witnesses to the centrality of the cross when he says:

> So when we preach that Christ was crucified, the Jews are offended, and the Gentiles say it's all nonsense. But to those called by God to salvation, both Jews and Gentiles, Christ is the mighty power of God and the wonderful wisdom of God. This "foolish" plan of God is far wiser than the wisest of human plans, and God's weakness is far stronger than the greatest of human strength. ... Dear brothers and sisters, when I first came to you I didn't use lofty words and brilliant ideas to tell you God's message. For I decided to concentrate only on Jesus Christ and his death on the cross.
> — 1 Corinthians 1:23-24; 2:1-2 NLT

One cannot talk about the work of this garden without talking about the cross. And talking about this garden and what happened there leads us to the fourth garden.

In the first garden, the Garden of Eden, we were introduced to the sin of humanity and the seed of salvation. The second garden, the desert garden, allowed us to see that seed in human form withstand the tests of Satan, and in the third garden, Gethsemane, we witnessed the titanic struggle of Jesus surrendering his will to the Father's, leading to the cross. Now we are about to enter the last garden.

Our Easter journey finally brings us to our gospel reading for this Easter Day. Jesus' body was requested by Joseph and Nicodemus. The request was granted by Pilate in an unusual turn of events because historically all crucifixion victims were not to be buried but their bodies left unattended for the animals to eat. Jesus' burial was, although I am sure Roman authorities would not admit it, an unofficial sign of Pilate's declaration of Jesus' innocence.

It is hard to think of a rock-strewn tomb as a garden, but it was. The empty tomb is an opportunity for us to visit the garden of life. This garden is not shackled by the forces of the past. All that limited Jesus in this natural order was destroyed with the crucifixion. Jesus' crucifixion was not an execution but rather it was liberation. Jesus now lives beyond the worst that can happen to him. I say that because the reality is that Jesus has faced death and is now alive, he is living beyond death!

What is the difference between life and resurrected life? Just think about it. You can kill life! Look at the cross and learn that even divine life could be killed. You cannot kill resurrection life. You cannot kill divine life that is on the other side of crucifixion. There is nothing that can touch that life. When you have risen from the dead, nothing can touch you!

When you have been hit by the worst possible circumstances and you rise in victory from out of the ashes, those former circumstances have lost their cutting edge. The power has been broken.

Nothing can stop Jesus Christ because he has ascended over death itself. There is no other enemy who is as great as death. Jesus Christ was slain by death but then he turned the tables, overcame death itself, and rose again. Death cannot ever touch him. Death is less than what Christ is. Crucifixion is less than what Christ is.

In the garden of the tomb the women were forever changed because they had talked with and experienced resurrection life. All they had been told was true and they were looking at the Messiah. Nothing would ever again deter them from praising his name. This same resurrection life would transform the disciples, and that resurrection life is here this morning — ready to transform all of us.

My sisters and brothers in Christ, we have all been to the first garden. We are all in need of repentance. Many of us have also traveled into the second garden, the garden of testing. At one time or another we all failed there as well. Only Jesus stood up to that test. Few of us show the maturity to go into the third garden, the garden of surrender and pain. And the fourth garden is beyond the reach of most — if not all of us.

But that garden is open to you today. The scriptures say today is the acceptable time for salvation. Easter tells us that the first and foremost reality is that suffering and death are not only enemies of life but a means of reminding us of life's twin realities, love and hate. Here, love and hate did not just happen. The paths were chosen. Those who hurt him hated him. Those who hated him, he loved. Those who killed him wanted to be rid of him and by allowing himself to be killed, he made it possible for them and all of us to live. Do you realize what this means to your life? In resurrection life you will be able to go forth in your walk with the Lord, higher up and deeper down. The Lord offers you the right to live by resurrection life. Resurrection life exists only as it is a life that has fully walked through the valley of the shadow of death that we call the crucifixion. Jesus awaits your permission to be crucified in the manner and style of Christ. That gives him permission to raise you from your spiritual grave and grant to you resurrected life. He is risen! He is risen indeed! Amen.

Should We Doubt Thomas?

John's gospel has traced the development of unbelief, which culminated in Jesus' enemies crucifying him. Conversely, John also traced the disciple's development of faith that was now coming to a head with doubting Thomas. You will remember that the disciples were affirming Jesus' resurrection to Thomas but Thomas was not buying it — not just yet. He wanted bodily proof of Jesus' risen state. The reappearance of Jesus a week later provided the opportunity Thomas wanted. Jesus miraculously entered a room with locked doors and asked Thomas to go ahead and touch him. This was a right-in-your-face challenge to Thomas.

Thomas' response to Jesus after having touched him is a high point of the gospel. I say that because Thomas was a skeptical man confronted by the evidence of Jesus' resurrection. He announced that Jesus is God in the flesh!

This Sunday after the Big Sunday — I want to spend a few minutes with the disciple history has named, often in a negative way, "Doubting Thomas."

First of all, I think we really need to ask ourselves is this doubt on the part of Thomas is to be viewed as a negative characteristic of Thomas himself, or should we see it as a positive attribute of this man? It seems that Thomas had an inquiring mind that needed to see the truth to believe what he had been told. We must remember that once he saw verification he was more than willing to believe the truth. Thomas, like any rational person, had questions and needed to have those questions answered. He just needed to see the truth for himself. You must admit you have questioned the resurrection yourself, and if you have not, let me suggest you have missed a meaningful part of your faith journey.

I think that the doubt Thomas expressed shows us how much he struggled with the questions of life and how honest a man he really was. Thomas wanted to know the truth and his doubt gives evidence of, not a lack of, faith — a desire to have a faith founded in fact, not hearsay.

I think it is instructive here to recognize that Thomas is mentioned more than once in John's gospel. We should consider that John is the only gospel writer that bothers to mention him at all, other than being listed as one of the disciples.

The first mention we find is in John 11:16. But let's look a bit earlier beginning at 11:7 and running through to verse 16:

> Finally after two days, he said to his disciples, "Let's go to Judea again." But his disciples objected. "Teacher," they said, "only a few days ago the Jewish leaders in Judea were trying to kill you. Are you going there again?" Jesus replied, "There are twelve hours of daylight every day. As long as it is light, people can walk safely. They can see because they have the light of this world. Only at night is there danger of stumbling because there is no light." Then he said, "Our friend Lazarus has fallen asleep, but now I will go and wake him up." The disciples said, "Lord, if he is sleeping, that means he is getting better!" They thought Jesus meant Lazarus was having a good night's rest, but Jesus meant Lazarus had died. Then he told them plainly, "Lazarus is dead. And for your sake, I am glad I wasn't there, because this will give you another opportunity to believe in me. Come, let's go see him." Thomas, nicknamed the Twin, said to his fellow disciples, "Let's go, too — and die with Jesus."
>
> — John 11:7-16 NLT

You may recall that the last few times that Jesus had been in Judea things had gotten a bit difficult. The Jews had tried to seize and kill Jesus so there was good reason why the disciples were not too eager to go back there to see Lazarus. However, here we see a good example of what Thomas is really made of. Thomas knew that Jesus was going back, no matter the possible consequences. Jesus was going to go to his dead friend Lazarus. The statement that Thomas makes here is a courageous one. He was willing to follow Jesus in this case even if it meant death. He was putting into action what Jesus had taught them when he said in Mark's gospel,

> Then he called his disciples and the crowds to come over and listen. "If any of you wants to be my follower," he told them, "you must put aside your selfish ambition, shoulder your cross, and follow me. If you try to keep your life for yourself, you will lose it. But if you give up your life for my sake and for the sake of the good news, you will find true life."
> — Mark 8:34-35 NLT

Thomas was willing to follow Jesus no matter what. He wanted to do the will of God and if this meant death then he was willing to take it. This doesn't sound like a man who is filled with doubt, a man who has questions with no answers. An honest appraisal here will tell us that Thomas, although he could see potential danger, was willing to go on, even in the face of death.

The second mention that we find of Thomas is in John 14:

> "Don't be troubled. You trust God, now trust in me. There are many rooms in my Father's home, and I am going to prepare a place for you. If this were not so, I would tell you plainly. When everything is ready, I will come and get you, so that you will always be with me where I am. And you know where I am going and

how to get there." "No, we don't know, Lord," Thomas said. "We haven't any idea where you are going, so how can we know the way?" Jesus told him, "I am the way, the truth, and the life. No one can come to the Father except through me."

— John 14:1-6 NLV

These verses from John once again show that Thomas is not satisfied with the easy answers to life's complex questions. It shows a side of Thomas that is so very much like we ourselves. How often have we tried to teach our children that when you do not know the answer to a question, never be ashamed to ask for clarification? So it seems that one of the most repeated statements ever uttered by our Lord was prompted by Thomas's honesty. Thomas is an inquiring mind. He was not satisfied with what others took for granted. And he was not afraid to say so. This is brought to such clarity when he says to Jesus that he really does not know how to get to where Jesus is saying he should go. "How can I know the way?" Is that not exactly the question we are asking by being a part of this community of faith?

Although the two readings we just went over do not help identify Thomas as a person of doubt, they do set the tone for what he said in our gospel reading for today. Let's look again at verses 24-29.

One of the disciples, Thomas (nicknamed the Twin), was not with the others when Jesus came. They told him, "We have seen the Lord!" But he replied, "I won't believe it unless I see the nail wounds in his hands, put my fingers into them, and place my hand into the wound in his side." Eight days later the disciples were together again, and this time Thomas was with them. The doors were locked; but suddenly, as before, Jesus was standing among them. He said, "Peace be with you." Then he said to Thomas, "Put your finger here and see my hands. Put your hand into the wound in my side. Don't be faithless any longer. Believe!" "My

Lord and my God!" Thomas exclaimed. Then Jesus told him, "You believe because you have seen me. Blessed are those who haven't seen me and believe anyway."

— John 20:24-29 NLT

It is easy to see where we get the nickname doubting Thomas because even Jesus says, "Don't be faithless any longer. Believe!" That was enough to birth the title, "Doubting Thomas."

For clarification, we need to take a quick glance at the whole story. We know that Mary Magdalene was the first witness to see Jesus. She then told the disciples. But when we see the first appearance of Jesus to the disciples, they were hidden away in the upper room — afraid they were next! Let's be honest, women were not exactly to be believed by the men. Here is the truth of the matter. Jesus first appeared to a former hooker and then she told this group of fairly typical Jewish men that their Lord was not really dead but that he had risen. You don't think they questioned what she was saying? I would think that there might have been some doubt in their minds and one of the only differences between Thomas and the rest of Jesus' followers is that Thomas had the guts to speak up.

Thomas was not with them when Jesus arrived and so he wanted some proof. He was not an eyewitness as were the others. There was doubt in his mind but I don't think it was a doubt in his Lord. Maybe it was a doubt in the others. Remember an entire week had passed when this happens. Thomas needed a faith founded on fact that he himself had discovered. He just could not take anyone's word for it but had to see for himself and when he did he did not doubt but was a very faithful disciple.

His reaction to the risen Christ is also very profound as he addresses him as God. He says, "My Lord and my God." A powerful truth comes out of Thomas here. He knew that when he saw the risen Lord, he truly was encountering God. I don't think that he would ever forget that.

I know at times we really can identify with Thomas. We have doubts and we want to know something for ourselves. Sometimes no one's word is good enough, we just need to see and know for ourselves. Is this not having faith? I don't think so. What faith is greater: the one that never doubts or the faith that doubts and investigates and believes? We see examples throughout history of people who doubted and some even went as far as to try to disprove Christ. Sometimes the people who doubt the most and then come to belief are the most energetic Christians and love to tell others about what they have found.

When we have doubts or when we hear about doubting Thomas, let's remember that he was so much more than a doubter. He was one who needed to find out for himself, needed to search for the truth, and needed to believe not because of other people's words but because God revealed it to him. We can trust others but let us search. Let us be like Thomas in his dedication to Christ, in his desire to really know for himself this risen Lord. I think Thomas really fits what Josh McDowell once said, "My heart cannot rejoice in what my mind rejects."

In closing I would go back to John 20:29, when Jesus told him, "You believe because you have seen me. Blessed are those who haven't seen me and believe anyway." The last sentence, the very last word, should leave the message embedded in our hearts. It should be clear in our memory. It should be received as simple, clear, and unforgettable. Who has the last word and what is it to be? Another gospel writer may have left things differently with some moralizing observation but not John. True to the inspiration that informed this gospel, that word has taken up residence in John's heart and soul, John gives the last word to the Good Shepherd who has laid down his life for his friends. The Son of God brings this story to its conclusion with his beatitude concerning spiritual seeing. Standing in the midst of his disciples in whom he had breathed his very self, he pronounces this once and for all blessing, "You believe because you have seen me. Blessed are those who haven't seen me and believe anyway."

And what is the ground for believing? John's entire gospel is a rejection of any ground of believing outside of Jesus himself. "Come and see" is Jesus' invitation to us all. Jesus stands in the middle of the disciples and Jesus stands in our midst as well and invites us all to join him in his ministry to the world. Truth be told, John's gospel is to be read and savored for us just as it was for Thomas who had questions.

This puts the Christian experience into proper perspective. It gives us in one short but succinct verse the whole message of John's gospel to us, "You believe because you have seen me. Blessed are those who haven't seen me and believe anyway." Amen.

What Is the Point?

What is the purpose of the church? Why was it established? What is the purpose against which we should measure everything we do?

Read: Luke 24:36-49.

One of the single most important things we need to notice in our reading this morning is what was the first matter of concern that Jesus dealt with when he was with his disciples following his resurrection. It was that Jesus felt the need to help them better understand that he had really been resurrected. Not only did he stand in their presence so they could see him and his wounds but he also ate food in front of them to show that he was not a ghost.

The second major item was helping them to better understand that all the things written about him in the Hebrew scriptures about the Messiah were accurate. The Law of Moses, the prophets and the psalms were all familiar to the disciples and Jesus showed them from different parts of these writings that he is the Messiah and that he must suffer and rise from the dead. Because of his death and resurrection, the message of repentance and forgiveness of sins could now be preached in his name to all the nations, beginning in Jerusalem. This in fact became the outline for Luke in the book of the Acts of the Apostles.

Finally in our closing verses to our reading Jesus commanded the disciples to remain in the city of Jerusalem until they had received power from on high, which was a clear reference to the coming of the Holy Spirit who had been promised.

So it seems quite clear from this passage that the mission Jesus left with his disciples was to proclaim repentance and forgiveness of sins in his name. The purpose assigned to his disciples, and ultimately the church, was to tell all of God's children that there was a better way to live a faithful life than the way the world had been teaching them. That way was, and is, the way of Jesus Christ.

It is really important that we remember and put into some kind of proper context just how the church developed following those early beginnings. In the first century, following the birth of the early church, there was an excitement and there was energy as Christians found their voice in the world. Those early Christians faced an often-hostile world with a real sense of hope that the people of the world would find what they had found in Jesus Christ. The church was vibrant and alive with purpose. The church was directed and focused and the church grew by leaps and bounds as people came to understand the message Jesus had left with his followers.

I guess I do not have to tell you that we no longer see that kind of growth in the church today. Far too many people think the church has little purpose in society today. The church is seen by many as a good place for a wedding, funeral, or the occasional baptism, but not for much else. We need to at least ask why in the world would anyone attend church today on a regular basis. Many believe that the church, by way of its teachings, serves to impose a narrow-minded intolerance upon people. The sad fact is that far too many people in the church are seen as an institution against things, instead of a body of believers that are for positive growth and positive ideas for the future.

When the world asks the question of the church, "What's the point?" many do not find a satisfactory answer. That is why it is imperative that we work our way through Lent and Easter and try to remember what it was that got people so excited, so dedicated, so spirit-filled. Taking the time to look into the answer will enable twenty-first-century Christians to at least be able to look at the questions in an objective way. One of the answers found in our gospel lesson for today is that what we need to say and do is to "share a message!" The message is that Jesus Christ lived and died so that humankind might know God and be assured of eternity! We have a purpose: to share the message of Christ!

Before the message can be shared there are things that need to be done. We have to make sure the message is clear and easily understood. Jesus told the eleven disciples that everything that had been written about him had to be fulfilled. Then he opened their minds so they could understand what he was talking about. The scriptures contained a clear message about what was to happen to Jesus: Jesus would suffer, die, and rise from the dead. It is here in the middle of their own confusion and pain that Jesus steps back into their lives and tells them what they need to do, not necessarily what they want to hear.

Sometimes I wonder how many people truly understand the message and its implications for them today. Jesus showed the disciples that you didn't have to be rich to enjoy life. He showed them you didn't have to be part of the cultural elite to make a difference. He showed them how to live a life that was full and meaningful. And as the resurrected Jesus stood in front of them, he showed them that not even death could hold him. Jesus brought a message of life.

In order to share a message those sharing must first have their minds opened to understand that message themselves. They not only have to accept the message they must also find a way to share that message to all who will listen.

Jesus said that "repentance and forgiveness of sins would be preached in his name." The Greek word translated "preached" is a word that would refer to a town crier, someone who announced the news like a Paul Revere type of person. The word means quite literally, "to proclaim." It seems God's strategy for sharing the message was for people to proclaim it. In order for the message to be shared, people must understand the message and the strategy for sharing it; then, with clear purpose in mind, they must proclaim the message.

No matter what you may think of Mormons or Jehovah's Witnesses you must commend them for going out every day of every week, door to door, sharing their message. Again whether you agree or disagree with their message, they do at least know what their message is. Sadly that cannot be said for many in the church today.

The church has a message that can change people's lives. Our purpose is to share that message of God's love, in order to make a difference in the lives of those who hear it. But we're doing a poor job of sharing the message. If I were to ask how many of you within the last year shared with someone how they could have a relationship with God and eternal life there would probably be very few hands raised. If I were to extend that to the last five years the result would probably not be much different. The sad truth is that for the great majority of those who count themselves as Christians, they have never shared that fact with anyone else. Those around them don't even know of their faith.

Many of our comic book heroes do the work of being a hero by keeping a very low profile. They have costumes that combined with the elements make them almost invisible. Heroes like Batman do their best work in the dark. They use the shadows and darkness as a shield that keeps them out of harm's way. Spiderman can seemingly travel throughout the city, clinging to the sides of enormous buildings without giving himself away. They are, for lack of a better term, "stealth" heroes. Everything they do they do for good, but they don't want to talk about it. Sadly that describes many people's faith. Many people have a stealth faith. Radar can't even pick it up. And no one around them knows they're Christians.

In a variety of ways my sermons over the weeks in Lent and now Easter have spoken to you on the subject of God's sovereignty. It is no accident that you are part of the family of which you are a part, it is no accident that you work where you work or that you have the friends you have. If you are a Christian, in God's sovereignty, God has established a relationship with you and now God wants you to share with those around you the news of God's gift of life through Jesus Christ. That is the purpose for which God created you. Proclaiming that message is the mission of the church.

Again, in order for the message to be shared, the message has to be understood. To be able to share that message in ways that make it clear, the people who are sharing that message must first find the power to properly communicate what needs to be said and what needs to be heard. Jesus told his disciples to stay in the city until they received the power from "on high." When the disciples began to share the message of life through Jesus Christ, they had incredible results. There were days when they saw thousands of people accept the message and establish a relationship with Jesus. But before they began sharing the message, God empowered them with his Holy Spirit. God's Spirit not only empowered the message they shared, the Spirit of God empowered their lives as well. When people saw the way the disciples lived, they saw proof of the message the disciples shared. The Spirit of God gave the disciples the courage they needed to speak. And it was that same Spirit of God that made them compassionate toward those in need, content with what they had. It was this same Spirit that made them people of the greatest integrity, people who sought after God, people who wanted to know and understand God and God's ways. It was this same Spirit that made them people who lived their lives by God's rule and found the greatest fulfillment because they followed God.

One of the most fun things I remember doing was driving a 1968 Corvette. One of my parishioners in a former parish owned a really beautiful "'68 Vet." Driving that car was sort of a dream come true for me. If I could have any car in the world I would want a Corvette. It's a guy thing, I think. But I think your car says something about you. What you drive says something about you. A Corvette says you're just plain cool. I drive a Kia, oh well!

But suppose someone gave me a free Corvette and I couldn't afford to put gas in it. Gas is what fuels the car. Without gas the car has no power. Without gas it sits in the driveway and no one ever knows how cool the owner is.

Without the power of the Holy Spirit of God, your faith will grow weak. God gives you the Spirit when you enter into that special relationship with him. The Spirit of God helps direct the way you live and respond to the world in which you live. When the human side of you says to get angry, the Spirit of God says to show compassion. When you look out only for yourself it is the Spirit of God that tells you, "Put others first." We must submit ourselves to the leading of God's Holy Spirit first. When God calls, we must listen and then respond.

The Spirit of God is the power by which we will have lives so full that others will fall all over themselves to find out what makes our lives different. They will want to hear about our faith. But without the spirit of God your faith is just sitting in the driveway. It's going nowhere.

Without the Spirit of God to make us bold, we will never share the message that others so desperately need to hear.

Sisters and brothers in Christ we really do have a purpose. Our gospel lesson tells us to share that message with others. That message is that Jesus came and lived, died, and rose from the dead so that we might have life in all its abundance.

We must understand that God's strategy is for each of us to share that message with those who will hear what we have to say. Finally we must be submitted to God's Holy Spirit so that our lives will reflect the fullness that God offers and so that we will be courageous enough to share the message with others.

Our prime directive as individuals and as a church is to be sharing the message of life in Christ with a lost world. As a church, it is our purpose and everything we do must be measured by it. Amen.

The Shepherd of Love

As we continue our Easter journey, we are presented with an image that has stood the test of time. It is an image of solace, comfort, and hope. It is an image that helps people to see Jesus not only in a positive light, but in the light that God created so we all can see the world as it really should be.

In the first five verses of this chapter of John's gospel, we are presented with the scene of a shepherd entering through a gate into a walled enclosure that has several flocks of sheep in one sheep pen. The enclosure, with stone walls, is guarded at night by a doorkeeper to prevent thieves and beasts of prey from entering and bringing harm to the sheep. The fact was that anyone who took the time to climb over that wall was up to no good. And it should be noted that the shepherd has a right to enter the sheep pen. The one watching the gate opens that gate for the shepherd. When the shepherd comes in, he calls his own sheep by name. You see, shepherds know their sheep well enough to give them names. As sheep hear the familiar sound of the shepherd's voice they go to him. The shepherd leads them out of the pen until the entire flock is assembled. And when he goes out into the fields the sheep follow him.

It is instructive and important to the gospel reading to understand that if a stranger enters the pen, the sheep will run away from him because his voice is not familiar. The point of this is simply to say that the shepherd, because he knows his sheep and because his sheep trust him, is able to pull the flock together and go out into the world. In the same way people come to God because God calls them. If the people have a relationship with God, they therefore trust God and will follow.

Having said this, the fact is that the lesson was missed by those who heard Jesus even though they did understand the relationship between the shepherd and the sheep. In their blindness they just could not see Jesus as the Good Shepherd. They were still looking for something else!

We need to remember that it was Jesus himself that developed the shepherd/sheep figure of speech that has in many ways defined how some see Jesus even today. The people who heard this form of description of Jesus would have understood that the shepherd would separate his flock from the other sheep as they go to pasture. Once they got close to their pasture and the enclosure that would hold them while they are in the fields, the shepherd took his place in the doorway and acted as a human gate. What is happening here is that the sheep depend on the shepherd for all of their needs. The spiritual meaning is that Jesus is the only gate by which people can enter into God's providence.

When Jesus said, "All who came before me are thieves and bandits; but the sheep did not listen to them" (v. 8 NRSV), he was referring to those leaders of the nation who did not really care about the spiritual good of the people, but only cared about themselves. However, in Jesus the shepherd, they will find security from enemies and the shepherd also provides for their daily needs.

Just prior to our verses for today, we have an image of the thieves who are false shepherds and care only about feeding themselves. They will do everything they can to steal and kill if necessary to get what they want. They do not care about the sheep they care about their own comfort. Jesus said of them, "All others who came before me were thieves and robbers. But the true sheep did not listen to them" (v. 8 NLT).

Enter Jesus who has come to help the sheep, Jesus gives life, and it is life that is not held back in any way but is offered freely and without condition. The message is clear, Jesus gives life; the thief takes it!

If you were to ask our children if they could be any animal, how many do you think would answer that they would want to be a sheep? My guess is that probably none would want to be a sheep. Most would want to be a lion, an elephant, or something pretty like an exotic bird.

Why is it that no one ever says they want to be a sheep? It is never a mascot of a sports team. But from the Christian perspective, it is often seen as a romantic or complimentary thought to who we are.

The truth of the matter is that the attributes of sheep are not many. There is nothing romantic or complimentary about sheep. They are not too bright and most would say that they are stupid and stubborn. I mean, be honest, have you ever seen a trained sheep at the circus? Come see the dancing elephants, funny monkeys, and trained sheep. They are simple-hearted, dirty, and wayward; they are not at all like the sheep we see in the advertisements for mattresses on television. They easily wander away and it seems they never learn from their mistakes. They are easily frightened and confused and are known to plunge off cliffs in their fear and confusion. They are defenseless, dependant, and constantly need guidance and protection.

It may not be complimentary to be a sheep but it is comforting to know we have a good shepherd to come and rescue us when we, like sheep, go astray. Remember "thy rod and thy staff."

There are so many positive things about the Good Shepherd that it is important to get the point across in our journey of faith that we who call ourselves Christian are happy to be members of the flock that Jesus has so carefully assembled. Why are we happy? We are happy because Jesus has developed the sheep and shepherd metaphor in a third way as well. You see, Jesus knew that when it got dark outside, danger was all around. Sometimes in our Hollywood image of Jesus and the land in which he lived we forget what it was like in reality. In biblical times wild animals roamed freely in the hills and valleys around Palestine. The life of the shepherd, despite the romantic images we have managed to put together in our Christmas stories, was a difficult and often violent way of life. Just take a walk back in time and see what we discover in 1 Samuel:

> But David persisted. "I have been taking care of my father's sheep," he said. "When a lion or a bear comes to steal a lamb from the flock, I go after it with a club and take the lamb from its mouth. If the animal turns on me, I catch it by the jaw and club it to death."
> — 1 Samuel 17:34-35

> "The Lord who saved me from the claws of the lion and the bear will save me from this Philistine!" Saul finally consented. "All right, go ahead," he said. "And may the Lord be with you!"
> — 1 Samuel 17:37 NLT

That does not sound like an easy job! And Jacob also experienced the labor and toil of being a good shepherd:

> Twenty years I have been with you, and all that time I cared for your sheep and goats so they produced healthy offspring. In all those years I never touched a single ram of yours for food. If any were attacked and killed by wild animals, did I show them to you and ask you to reduce the count of your flock? No, I took the loss! You made me pay for every animal stolen from the flocks, whether the loss was my fault or not. I worked for you through the scorching heat of the day and through cold and sleepless nights.
> — Genesis 31:38-40 NLT

Once again we see how important it is that we understand just how much power titles can communicate. Jesus is the Good Shepherd and that says so much. In the Hebrew scriptures God is referred to as a shepherd; just recite the opening lines of Psalm 23. Well, Jesus is this to the Christian community and he came to give his life for the benefit of the sheep.

There are some facets of this Good Shepherd imagery that need to be more fully investigated. The Good Shepherd, Jesus, sacrifices everything for the sheep. Once again, he feeds them, cares for them, protects them, and is willing to die for them. Contrast this with the person paid to do the job. That person does not have the same kind of life commitment. That person is interested in making money and in taking care of number one. Hey, I am not saying that is always a bad thing. But if a wolf attacks the sheep what do you think the underpaid shepherd is going to do? He is going to run for his life. Obviously that shepherd cares nothing for the welfare of the sheep. Historically Israel had many false prophets, selfish kings, and pretenders to the throne when it came to an actual messiah. And the historic truth is that the flock of God suffered greatly from this kind of abuse.

The difference between the hired hand and the Good Shepherd is that the Good Shepherd has an intimate relationship with the flock. He has a personal interest in the well being of the sheep. Again, he knows them by name. Further because he knows the sheep by name they come to know him in the same way. The relationship is reciprocal. This kind of intimacy is modeled on the loving and trusting that comes from a mutual relationship between the Good Shepherd and God the Father. Jesus' care and concern is most clearly articulated by his willingness to die for the flock! I am sure that it can be said that some shepherds have died while protecting their sheep from danger. However,

Jesus willingly gave his life for his sheep and the fact is that his death gives them life!

Add to all of this the fact that the sheep are not one homogenous group. There are other sheep that are in need of the care that only the Good Shepherd can give.

> I have other sheep, too, that are not in this sheepfold. I must bring them also, and they will listen to my voice; and there will be one flock with one shepherd."
> — John 10:16 NLT

Jesus is referring to the Gentiles here. The power of his coming death would also bring these other sheep into the flock. They too will listen to what Jesus has to say. Jesus continues to bring people together to listen and to learn and finally to commit themselves to a new way of living, a new way of life. This seeking out of all who would listen compliments the growth of the early church. Jesus' message crossed over many flocks and many pastures on its way to finding itself in the life of the world. The evidence is widespread, just listen to the impact that message had when, one night the Lord spoke to Paul in a vision and told him,

> "Don't be afraid! Speak out! Don't be silent! For I am with you, and no one will harm you because many people here in this city belong to me." So Paul stayed there for the next year and a half, teaching the word of God.
> — Acts 18:9-11 NLT

In just another couple of weeks we will celebrate Pentecost and there you can see that Pentecost itself is a very direct result of the Good Shepherd doing what good shepherds do. They cared for their own flock and by so doing insured that other flocks would find their way into his safe and life-giving pastures.

In our closing verses today, Jesus predicted his death, saying no less than four times that he would voluntarily lay down his life. We can see as we absorb the totality of these verses that God has a special love for Jesus because of Jesus' sacrificial obedience to the will of God. Jesus predicted his death on more than one occasion. He predicted his resurrection on two occasions. It is so important that we understand that Jesus went forth into the world knowing what was going to happen and still he carried his own cross. The Good Shepherd was willing to die for the sheep, all of the sheep. The important point to be made is this, "No one can take my life from me. I lay down my life voluntarily. For I have the right to lay it down when I want to and also the power to take it again. For my Father has given me this command" (John 10:18 NLT).

The following is from Sir George Adam Smith:

> With us sheep are often left to themselves; but I do not remember ever to have seen in the East a flock of sheep without a shepherd. In such a landscape as Judea, where a day's pasture is thinly scattered over an unfenced tract of country covered with delusive paths, still frequented by wild beasts, and rolling off into the desert, the man and his character are indispensable. On some high moor, across which at night the hyenas howl, when you meet him, sleepless, far-sighted, weather beaten, armed, leaning on his staff, and looking out over his scattered sheep, everyone of them on his heart, you understand why the shepherd of Judea sprang to the forefront of his people's history; why they gave his name to their king and made him the symbol of providence; why Christ took him as the type of self-sacrifice.[1]

It is good to be reminded that our word "pastor" is Latin for "shepherd." It is, therefore, a highly suggestive term. It places every minister who leads a church under the high obligation of loving and nourishing the flock they serve. It summons every member to follow and feed and grow. Finally, the shepherd does not have the lambs; the sheep do. In other words just as Jesus has defined ministry through his thoughts, actions, and deeds, ministry is a collective endeavor and the entire flock must work together for the Good Shepherd. We have a promise fulfilled at the empty tomb that the Good Shepherd will always be with us. Amen.

---

1. George Adam Smith, *The Historical Geography of the Holy Land* (New York: Richard R. Smith, Publisher, 1894), 312-13.

Are We Withering on the Vine?

Jesus made pronouncement statements in John's gospel. They are commonly referred to as the "I am" statements. They are:

> 1. Jesus replied, "I am the bread of life. No one who comes to me will ever be hungry again. Those who believe in me will never thirst" (John 6:35 NLT).
> 2. Jesus said to the people, "I am the light of the world. If you follow me, you won't be stumbling through the darkness, because you will have the light that leads to life" (John 8:12 NLT).
> 3. Yes, I am the gate. Those who come in through me will be saved. Wherever they go, they will find green pastures (John 10:9 NLT).
> 4. Jesus told her, "I am the resurrection and the life. Those who believe in me, even though they die like everyone else, will live again" (John 11:25 NLT).
> 5. Jesus told him, "I am the way, the truth, and the life. No one can come to the Father except through me" (John 14:6 NLT).

The last is a part of our text for today, "I am the true vine, and my Father is the vinegrower." In the verses for the Fifth Sunday of Easter Jesus instructs his disciples on three important relationships. First, disciples are to be related to Jesus in the right way. Second, they are to be related to the world in the same way. Finally, they are to remain faithful and help one another.

I have two plants that live in my office. One of them is better than twenty years old. The other is only a few years old. If I do not pay attention to them, they do something that makes them look sad. They droop! They almost look as if they are going to cry. When I see them looking that way I immediately pay special attention to them by getting some water and better light for them. Within a very short period of time they look almost like they did when I first set them on the windowsill years ago.

I think it is fair to say that like our plants we wither from time to time. I am speaking of course about our walk with the Lord. Most people who identify themselves as Christians have very pronounced highs and lows in their journey of faith.

Generally speaking it is because we allow our relationship with Jesus to grow old, or like our plants, we forget to get the kind of nutrition that we need to stay fresh and vital. There are so many people who join the church, sign up for boards or committees, get excited for a week or two, and then everything gets old. For others it takes longer; maybe a couple of months, maybe a year, two years, or maybe even five years. What do I mean when I say it gets old?

I mean that our spiritual energy withers. Like drooping plants our relationship with Christ that was once so vibrant and fresh and exciting becomes slow, stale, and boring... dry! The sad thing is that sometimes it's hard to see this happening because these people still come to church, they still "do ministry," they still say all the right words, they still sing the hymns with gusto, and for most people looking in from the outside, all appears to be well.

When looked at in its historical context we can discern the fruit that God desired from Israel was for the people of Israel to be more loving, to show obedience to God, and to practice righteousness and justice in how they conducted their lives. When we take that idea and transport it through

Jesus, then in and through the disciples, and finally into all of us we begin to see how important it is for us to stay connected to Jesus who is the source of our Christian life.

The truth of the matter is that as human beings, it's easy to get disconnected from the vine. It's easy to let the ways of the world get hold of us and drain our obedience and the fruit that obedience to Jesus produces. That's why the advertising gurus on Madison Avenue always have to come out with new ads for new products, because we don't like seeing the same thing again and again. They know, and Jesus knew, that we like to be entertained and we are easily bored. This is why Jesus says in John 15:4, "Remain in me, and I will remain in you." If your relationship with Christ is to be fresh, if it is to be vibrant and exciting, it must remain connected to him. Otherwise we become like a branch that cannot produce fruit any longer and that branch is thrown into the fire. Every year Palestinian grape growers prune their vines. They cut off the dead wood that has no life in it and trim the living branches so that the yield will be greater. The people who first heard Jesus tell this story knew exactly what he was talking about. He says in verse 6, "If anyone does not remain in me, he is like a branch that is thrown away and withers; such branches are picked up, thrown into the fire and burned" (RSV).

Jesus understood our human nature, he knew that we get bored easily and he also knew that when we're bored we don't do anything well!

In this passage that refers to producing fruit in our lives, Jesus is getting to the heart of what prevents us from producing good fruit as Christians. Fruitfulness is the result of the Son's life being reproduced in a disciple. The disciple's part is to remain connected to the source of life. The word "remain," a key word in John's theology, is *meno*, which occurs eleven times in this chapter and forty times in the entire gospel and 27 times in John's letters. So, what does it mean to "remain"? It can mean to first accept Jesus as Savior. Secondly and just as importantly it can mean to continue or persevere in believing. Third, it can also mean believing, loving obedience. Without faith, without the life of God, no real fruit can be produced.

A disciple needs to be continually connected to Jesus if they intend to be the kind of strong fruit-bearing vine Jesus is looking for. It is really not that complicated. A branch without life is dead and needs to be cut off the vine so it will not hurt the other healthy parts of the plant. As usual Jesus is using language that is filled with visual effects. Those hearing what Jesus said then and now should be able to see that the burned branches are Christians who have lost their way. The burned branches represent Christians who will lose their standing with Jesus because of their willful separation from him — like Judas! It is clear that Jesus is also saying here that a burned branch, a person without Christ, is spiritually dead.

Remember Judas was with Jesus, he sure seemed to be connected but he did not have God's life in him and because of that he separated himself from Jesus and in so doing denied himself the opportunity to come into the kingdom. It isn't that difficult to know when your relationship with Christ has grown tired and disconnected from him. It begins when you start to wither. You know you're withering when you go to church because you feel guilty if you don't go, not because you want to go; it begins when you read your Bible like it is a catalog instead of a love letter addressed to you; when your praying becomes a habit instead of an honest heart to heart with God, and when your worship is reduced to sitting in the pew and counting the minutes until you hear the benediction and can go home.

There are many things that can cause us to become weak in our relationship with Jesus. It may be that you are fading because you are too comfortable and your comfort makes you lazy and out of touch. That is what happened with the people Israel.

> But that is the time to be careful! Beware that in your plenty you do not forget the Lord your God and disobey his commands, regulations, and laws. For when you have become full and prosperous and have built fine homes to live in, and when your flocks and herds have become very large and your silver and gold have multiplied along with everything else that is the time to be careful. Do not become proud at that time and forget the Lord your God, who rescued you from slavery in the land of Egypt.
> — Deuteronomy 8:11-14 NLT

God loves to bless God's people and a lot of us like to receive that blessing. But sometimes we forget the blessings God has bestowed upon us. There are a lot of people in our world who are spiritually weak because they have too much comfort — they've been blessed with everything they need and more.

You all know that regardless of how your life seems to be going, there is always something to be thankful for. There is always a reason to look to God and be happy because you know that you are blessed. It may be something so common that you forget to be thankful. How about the air you breathe? How about the fact that you have clothes on your back and a roof over your head? Even those who find themselves in difficult circumstances can know that regardless of those circumstances your God still loves you and is always there for you. The truth is that gratitude to God needs to come from your heart because it is a part of your life, a part of your everyday living.

The truth of the matter is that sometimes people have to become uncomfortable in order to break free from being held hostage with too much of everything. Have you ever noticed that more people turn to God when there is tragedy than when everything is going well? You see, when you're uncomfortable then you realize that you need God!

Maybe that's why Jesus said in Matthew 5:3-4 (NRSV), "Blessed are the poor in spirit, for theirs is the kingdom of heaven. Blessed are those who mourn, for they will be comforted."

You can begin to wither when you get too comfortable with the same thing all the time. Variety just may be the spice of life. Change can be the engine that propels you into the kind of disciple Jesus wants you to be.

It's true that some habits are good but it is equally true that some habits are bad. For example it is a good habit when you have a regular devotional time with God. It is a bad habit when that's the only reason you have a regular devotional time with God. Do you meet with God out of habit or out of love?

Do you come to church out of habit? Do you say "Amen" out of habit? Do you say, "I'll pray for you!" out of habit? Do you say, "Lord, forgive me" out of habit? Do you say, "I love you Jesus," out of habit? If any of these fit you then you're withering because you're too habitual. You are not connected to the source of inspiration and hope that you need! You need to break some habits and the only way you're going to break them is if you're aware of them. When we start to do things out of habit then we start to grow distant from God.

It may just be that you are withering because you are too judgmental when you need to be more forgiving. Here is a reminder from Jesus to us all this morning.

> Stop judging others and you will not be judged. For others will treat you as you treat them. Whatever measure you use in judging others, it will be used to measure how you are judged. And why worry about a speck in your friend's eye when you have a log in your own? How can you think of saying, "Let me help you get rid of that speck in your eye," when you can't see

past the log in your own eye? Hypocrite! First get rid of the log from your own eye; then perhaps you will see well enough to deal with the speck in your friend's eye.

— Matthew 7:1-5 NLT

We must recognize that people who are too judgmental have a very hard time forgiving people. Generally speaking those who cannot forgive cannot see the problems that live in their own lives. In the end those who find it hard to forgive people will become bitter people and bitter people are people who have lost their spiritual connection to the vine.

The truth is that we are all fooling ourselves if we think for a minute that we can be in Christ while we are filled with indifference and apathy and hate. We cannot!

If we are going to be honest with ourselves we have to admit that one of the most glaring reasons people wither on the vine is because of being too indolent. You need to be full of Christ and therefore full of the Spirit and filled with the kind of energy that makes you an excited and exciting Christian.

Here is a way of understanding laziness that comes to us from Chuck Swindoll.

> Let's pretend that you work for me. In fact, you are my executive assistant in a company that is growing rapidly. I'm the owner and I'm interested in expanding overseas. To pull this off, I make plans to travel abroad and stay there until a new branch office gets established. I make all the arrangements to take my family and move to Europe for six to eight months. And I leave you in charge of the busy stateside organization. I tell you that I will write you regularly and give you directions and instructions. I leave and you stay. Months pass. A flow of letters are mailed from Europe and received by you at the national headquarters. I spell out all my expectations. Finally, I return. Soon after my arrival, I drive down to the

office and I am stunned. Grass and weeds have grown up high. A few windows along the street are broken. I walk into the receptionist's room. She is doing her nails, chewing gum, and listening to her favorite disco station. I look around and notice the wastebaskets are overflowing. The carpet hasn't been vacuumed for weeks, and nobody seems concerned that the owner has returned. I asked about your whereabouts and someone in the crowded lounge area points down the hall and yells, "I think he's down there." Disturbed, I move in that direction and bump into you as you are finishing a chess game with our sales manager. I ask you to step into my office, which has been temporarily turned into a television room for watching afternoon soap operas. "What in the world is going on, man?"

"What do you mean, Darren?" "Well, look at this place! Didn't you get any of my letters?" "Letters? Oh yes! Sure! I got every one of them. As a matter of fact, Darren, we have had a letter study every Friday since you left. We have even divided the personnel into small groups to discuss many of the things you wrote. Some of the things were really interesting. You will be pleased to know that a few of us have actually committed to memory some of your sentences and paragraphs. One or two memorized an entire letter or two — great stuff in those letters." "Okay. You got my letters. You studied them and meditated on them; discussed and even memorized them. But what did you do about them?" "Do? We didn't do anything about them."

(*Improving Your Serve*, Chuck Swindoll)

The truth of the matter is that some of us get too sluggish to really do anything for God. If we really want to have an exciting relationship with Christ then we need to be available and we need to open ourselves to new ways of serving our Lord. Slothfulness can be a hindrance in our being an effective witness for Christ.

Having said that it may just be that you are withering not because you are too lazy but because you are too busy! Some of us get so busy that we miss out on the things God is saying to us. When our "business" interferes with our relationship with God then that relationship will suffer. If you ever seek out and find an excuse for not spending time in prayer or spending time reading the Bible or going to church then you are just too busy.

No one can follow Jesus on his or her own terms. Jesus defined through his preaching, teaching, and personal example what we need to do if we want to be his disciple. It is instructive to remember that the word "disciple" means learner. When we accept that name we do not declare ourselves to be saints. What we have said is that we go to school with Jesus. We learn from him. We start as little children, we mature and grow into adulthood, and along the way we will stumble. But we are always instructed to abide in him.

In closing listen to these words from Hebrews, "When the ground soaks up the rain that falls on it and bears a good crop for the farmer, it has the blessing of God. But if a field bears thistles and thorns, it is useless. The farmer will condemn that field and burn it" (Hebrews 6:7-8 NLT).

Are you drinking in the rain that God is showering on you and are you enjoying the blessings that God has given you? Are you enjoying the blessings that have provided you with a meaningful and exciting relationship with Christ? Or are you like a thirsty plant that is withering because you are just too comfortable and have forgotten who's providing the rain? Are you so habitual that you have forgotten how to open yourself to become fruitful soil that produces good and helpful fruit? Have you become so judgmental that the rain God provides simply runs off your back? Or have you become so lazy that your soil has turned to clay and water can no longer feed the good fruit? Is it possible that you have become so busy that the rain cannot even touch you?

Jesus is able to provide all you need to help you remain a healthy and productive part of the vine. "Yes, I am the vine; you are the branches. Those who remain in me, and I in them, will produce much fruit. For apart from me you can do nothing." Amen.

Living a Joyful Life

Throughout this Easter season we have talked about the importance of staying connected to Jesus even when that connection means trouble. Obviously the journey to the cross and the view from that cross has provided us with an often disturbing and at the same time hopeful look at what it will mean to be called a disciple of the Christ. It is evident that Jesus took great joy in pleasing God by living a fruitful life and passing that fruitful life along to his followers. So the commands for those who choose to follow Jesus are given for their joy.

I want to draw our attention today to verse 11 from our reading, "I have told you this so that you will be filled with my joy. Yes, your joy will overflow!" (John 15:11 NLT).

As I read that verse, it reminds me that when Jesus Christ wants to do anything in us and for us, he doesn't stop with halfway measures. He does not just want to give us joy he wants to make sure we are filled with that joy. Joy is anything that brings us delight, happiness, and even wonder. From the First Sunday in Lent and continuing right through today's message, some form of joy has been present, even in the most difficult of circumstances. Remember that Jesus said one of the reasons he was who he was and did what he did was so that we could live life more abundantly. When he speaks of joy, he is speaking of something far different than the understanding we tend to read into this of just being happy. As was stated a moment ago, joy has more than one meaning. For lack of another way of putting it, joy for Jesus is the difference between living life and living that life the way it should be lived.

Another way of putting it would be to say that happiness in our lives, and therefore in our ministries, tends to be based on circumstances that are often beyond our control. But joy is often present despite difficult circumstances.

The world in which we live is often defined by "stuff." By that I mean that we have become a nation of possessions. For some people those possessions may be visual: a new car, nice home, and fashionable clothing. For others the most important possession is wealth and for far too many people the acquisition of more property or wealth is a continuous struggle. They become defined by that struggle. Usually when these same people get that one more thing, whatever that thing may be, they are no more satisfied than they were before getting whatever it was they were seeking. For many people the belief that more stuff brings you happiness is based upon the false notion that possessions can reduce anxiety, fear, and worry. They certainly can make you feel good for a while but in and of themselves they have no real healing properties at all. In the end they are objects, plain and simple.

I read a statement by William Lyon Phelps that sums it up: "If happiness were based on ease and freedom from worry, the happiest individual in the world would be an American cow." The joy Christ offers is not based on fleeting circumstances, having its sure foundation in Christ the rock and the promises of God. So we find a definition for joy not in abundance of possessions or ease of living but in something which sees beyond and reaches beyond those things. For those who have found true joy, we find powerful statements of faith like this one:

> Even though the fig trees have no blossoms, and there
> are no grapes on the vine; even though the olive crop

fails, and the fields lie empty and barren; even though the flocks die in the fields, and the cattle barns are empty, yet I will rejoice in the Lord! I will be joyful in the God of my salvation.

— Habakkuk 3:17-18 NLT

Think what those circumstances meant to an Israelite of biblical times. With no crops in the fields and no flocks in the stalls, the writer is basically saying, "I have been devastated." Yet he speaks of joy in the Lord. Joy will carry us beyond all our circumstances.

Someone once said that "happiness tends to lift the emotions while joy lifts the soul." This is an observation that is much easier seen than put into words but we know it when we see it. We have all known people who can seem to be filled to overflowing with happiness one minute and the next they are filled with anxiety. However, we have all known people who, despite lousy circumstances, seem to be filled to overflowing with real joy that seems to come from deep within their souls.

Observing someone with this joy that seems to manifest itself despite what is going on around them can be a wonderful life lesson. Usually the main difference between people filled with real joy and those who only have that surface sort of joy is found in the person's ability to share that joy with others. Mother Teresa said, "A person filled with joy preaches without preaching." I have found this to be so true. Just look at how she was able to radiate a genuine sense of joy despite working in circumstances that most of us would find appalling. It is easy to see why people who came in contact with Mother Teresa walked away with their souls lifted and their spirits high. That is what I think of when I think of joy as opposed to happiness: joy will not be restrained it will always overflow and lift others.

It follows then that more often than not happiness happens, while our sense of joy is something we choose for our lives. The message to us from the earliest leaders of our country is the wonderful notion that all of us should, at a basic level, be able to find ourselves in the "pursuit of happiness." But no matter what the well intentioned idea was of pursuing that happiness, finding it has often proved to be elusive. Nathaniel Hawthorne said, "Happiness is a butterfly, which, when pursued, is always just beyond your grasp, but which, if you will sit down quietly, may alight upon you." Happiness on its own end seems to be very elusive indeed. Joy seems to have different origins and is looking for a different result. Abraham Lincoln said, "Most folks are about as happy as they make up their minds to be." As usual, honest Abe seems to have hit the nail squarely on the head. I believe he spoke more about what I define as joy, a deeper and more settled form of happiness. Happiness seems to result from some physical event or circumstance that produces the feeling of happiness; but joy is happiness that has found its true center.

The great C.S. Lewis said that God designed the human machine to run on himself. He himself is the fuel our spirits were designed to burn or the food our spirits were designed to feed on. There is no other. That is why it is just so good asking God to make us happy in our own way without bothering about religion. God cannot give us a happiness and peace apart from himself, because it is not there. There is no such thing.[1]

Lewis seems to be saying that there is no happiness apart from our connection to God. And if our happiness comes from anything other than God it will not last and will not have the desired effect we want for our lives.

There is an important distinction to be made here. Happiness tends to focus on "things" but joy focuses on people, individually and collectively as in the church. Look again: "I have told you this so that you will be filled with my joy. Yes, your joy will overflow!" (John 15:11 NLT).

Jesus is saying that he has told us the things he has said so that we might be filled with joy. If you look back at this and other chapters you will find that the focus of the teachings Jesus has shared with us through John's gospel are all about how we do or do not "abide" in the love offered by him to us. The message is filled throughout with the proclamation that Jesus is the very source of our joy. Whatever joy we internalize apart from him will leave us feeling empty. Our fullness of joy will come in direct correlation to our ability not to allow the world to interfere with our staying focused on Jesus and Jesus only.

So we come to the conclusion that happiness is more often connected with our getting something while joy seems to find its life in being given away! If we go through life spending all our efforts on getting stuff we think will bring us happiness, we are going to be disappointed. Sadly, in current times almost everything that seems to be of value is time stamped. By that I mean that be it a new computer or a new iPad, its newness, its technological wonders, will last only a short period of time. They are designed to be quick fixes and they are built to fill a void but only for a short period of time. Those who rely on the latest technology are often the people with very short attention spans and that lack of patience is exactly what the manufacturers want. They want you to be happy, albeit for only a short period of time. They do not want you filled with joy.

Our wanting to have things to make us happy can, and often does, become an obsession. In the end, we usually find that those things we think will become the happiness we are seeking will not make us happy over the long run. It seems all of life has become a sprint and not a marathon. You know the story of the turtle and the hare. We need to be more like the turtle. Being careful may slow us down but we will always stay in the race and continue to seek joy in our lives.

One of the most time tested television and movie titles were those created by Gene Roddenberry, *Star Trek* being the preeminent of his many works. Those of you who became *Star Trek* fans, or Trekkies, will be familiar with the character, Mr. Spock. Mr. Spock was a Vulcan and as such he was able to keep his emotions in check and use only logic to solve problems. The word happiness or feeling of happiness would not have fit into his life. He did, however, have an ability to understand how emotions affected the human ability to function well. Mr. Spock said the following, "There seems to be more satisfaction in *wanting* than in *having*, it is illogical but it is true."

Even Jesus did not suggest that there was no joy in receiving but Jesus did say, "It is more blessed to give than to receive." The difference is like the difference at Christmas between opening presents you have received and watching someone else open a gift that you have given them. They both produce a happy response but the feeling produced by having given is of a much deeper quality.

It seems that our Lord wants us to understand that happiness is made manifest in the things that we can see while joy focuses on that which cannot be seen. The apostle Paul said that the only way for us to be able to focus on what is eternal can happen only when "we do this by keeping our eyes on Jesus, on whom our faith depends from start to finish. He was willing to die a shameful death on the cross because of the joy he knew would be his afterward. Now he is seated in the place of highest honor beside God's throne in heaven" (Hebrews 12:2 NLT). His message is to remember that visible things may give us happiness but true joy seems always to have its origins in the invisible.

We are to focus our attention, not on that which seems to give immediate gratification but to look beyond that to Jesus, who was able to take that journey to Calvary, knowing what joy lay before him. One might rightly ask where in the world did the author of Hebrews ever see any joy being set before Jesus. All that ever lay before him in this life was a road that took him to pain, suffering, and death. That's because the joy that was set before him was an unseen joy.

Jesus kept his eyes focused on the will of God and the good that would result from his perfect sacrifice. Because of that sacrifice we who would follow him now can look at the world through "resurrection eyes." We can, because of Jesus' life, death, and resurrection, be filled with the joy that came from sacrifice. We can, as it has been said before, "walk the walk and talk the talk," because Jesus has already made the pathway passable. Because we are able to see with eyes other than the physical ones we see the world with, we are able to see and understand with resurrection eyes that the journey of joy must necessarily be a journey of faith. It is only by faith that we can be joyful in spite of our circumstances, it is only by faith that we can make joy a daily choice, it is only by faith that we get our focus off of the world of physical things and onto Jesus the source of our joy, and it is only by faith that we can see the invisible beyond the visible. "I have told you this so that you will be filled with my joy. Yes, your joy will overflow!" (John 15:11). Amen.

---

1. C.S. Lewis, *Mere Christianity*, book 11 (New York: Macmillan Publishing Company, Inc.), 54.

Reflections of a Healthy Church

Ascension Day is a good time for the Christian community to assess where it has been and where it is going. We need to ask ourselves why we are here and exactly what is it we are supposed to be doing. Our lesson for this day provides us with much needed information on what we should be doing and what our final destination as we travel this road in ministry with Jesus is.

In order to gain the full impact of our verses for today we need first to take a quick look at those that have preceded them. In verses 36-43, Jesus proved beyond all doubt to those who followed him that he had really been resurrected. Not only did he stand in their presence so they could actually lay eyes on him but he also ate food in front of them to show them that he was real and not a ghost. They were overwhelmed, as we all should be as we participate in the story as it is told in Luke's gospel. Before Jesus returned to his rightful place in heaven there were some final things he wanted to do for his disciples. First of all he wanted to turn their panic into hope and that hope into a church. His presence with them scared them at first and so he looked upon them and said, "Peace, be with you." The one they had followed and loved has returned. He stood before them offering them peace of mind and heart, and a new hope for the future.

All people in all places look for the things that will bring peace in their lives. We all know that the world offers all kinds of false fixes to help people find peace of mind. It may be too much alcohol, too many drugs, or just too much of too much! But sooner or later these temporary fixes fail the test of time. And when they do fail, it often leaves us feeling worse than we did in the first place. Just think of all the effort that is put into these quick fixes to life. When these things do not do what was expected we become emotionally unhinged and confused as to just what we should do.

It is then that Jesus steps into the void and turns confusion into hope-filled clarity. Often as Jesus taught the disciples they did not truly understand what it was he was trying to tell them. We can see this in Luke 9:45 where we read, "But they didn't know what he meant. Its significance was hidden from them so they could not understand it and they were afraid to ask him about it." We can see how important it was to Jesus and how important it was to the disciples that at this time, in this place, they would know what was about to happen. Jesus was not taking any chances here and wanted to make sure there was no more confusion.

Have you ever been confused? I mean really confused! You may be like the university student I heard about. A university student was seen with a large "K" printed on his T-shirt. When someone asked him what the "K" stood for, he said, "Confused." "But," the questioner replied, "You don't spell confused with a K." The student answered, "You don't know how confused I am."

Jesus helped the disciples to turn their confusion onto clarity; to turn their lack of direction into something workable; to help them in discovering the purpose behind their relationship with him. It seems that the real problem for the disciples at that time and the real problem for all of us is that our confusion can quickly turn into a lack of purpose and then a deliberate turning away from what Jesus has taught us as we have traveled with him to this point in our journey of faith. Jesus says to them, "And now I will send the Holy Spirit, just as my Father promised. But stay here in the city until the Holy Spirit comes and fills you with power from heaven" (Luke 24:49 NLT).

The problem then, as it is today, is that the disciples had become so inwardly focused they had forgotten their purpose. This fact should be a wake-up call to the church today. Lack of direction and purpose is often the reason people leave the church or worse yet a reason they never find themselves involved in church at all. The only good news in all of this is that we know it is not new. Luke, writing in the book of the Acts of the Apostles reminds them, "But when the Holy Spirit has come upon you, you will receive power and will tell people about me everywhere — in Jerusalem, throughout Judea, in Samaria, and to the ends of the earth" (Acts 1:8 NLT).

We can see that the direction and purpose of the church has not changed over time. We are to be doing the same thing as the church when it was first formed. We are to proclaim a message of repentance, forgiveness, and love to the waiting world. It is a message that supersedes time and space. It is a message that says, and I paraphrase a motto of the United Church of Christ that says, "No matter who you are or where you are in life's journey, you are welcome here." And the "here" is the church of Jesus Christ.

The problem for us today is in getting that message out to a waiting world. It is the "e" word that is the problem. That "e" word is of course evangelism. Most people think that telling people about Jesus is the job of the pastor or at the very least some of the more outgoing and gregarious members of the church. Most of us just do not feel qualified to be a gospel messenger. But that is a mistake and a big one!

The word "evangelize" is used 54 times in the New Testament, evangel or gospel is used 76 times, and evangelist is used three times. These are good words. They are biblical words. We are told by Jesus himself that we are to be the ones who do the work of the evangelist. We can evangelize the world.

When we take the time to look at the varying ways in which we have been told to do this work of evangelism we come away with a sense of just how important this ministry is to the overall health of the church. Think for a moment of the various figurative representations used in the person and work of the Holy Spirit. The Spirit is described as: a dove in Matthew 3:6, a seal in Ephesians 1:13, oil in Hebrews 1:9, fire in Acts, rain in Zechariah, wind in John 3:8, a river in John 7:38, dew in Isaiah 18:4, and clothing in our gospel lesson for today. The point is that we have been given so much in terms of how we might go about describing the power and majesty of Jesus Christ that there really is no good excuse for our not doing exactly what we know we are to do.

The ministry that we call evangelism is a group enterprise when we are talking about how the task of evangelizing the world can be accomplished. It is true that not every single person is cut out to be knocking on doors proclaiming Jesus Christ is Lord. Not everyone is gifted as an evangelist, but there is always something that every church member can do in the work of evangelizing. In light of the ways that the power of the Holy Spirit is described throughout scripture it should be no surprise that there is somewhere and something for everyone to do in the church of Jesus Christ.

That should be a liberating notion to those who feel threatened by not being able to speak in public.

Our journey from Ash Wednesday to Easter has shown us that Jesus was anointed to preach good news to the poor, to proclaim release to the captives, recovery of sight to the blind, and to set at liberty those who are oppressed. That is the work of those who want to follow Jesus in their own lives. The good news is that we like Paul and the disciples of old can be servants of the ultimate servant to all, even Jesus who is Christ.

We must be like Paul, when he said, "For I am not ashamed of this good news about Christ. It is the power of God at work, saving everyone who believes — Jews first and also Gentiles." This good news tells us how God makes us right in his sight. This is accomplished from start to finish by faith. As the scriptures say, "It is through faith that a righteous person has life" (Romans 1:16-17 NLT).

The witness of the early church was not based on the empty tomb but on the encounter of the disciples with the risen Lord.

> I passed on to you what was most important and what had also been passed on to me — that Christ died for our sins, just as the scriptures said. He was buried, and he was raised from the dead on the third day, as the scriptures said. He was seen by Peter and then by the twelve apostles. After that, he was seen by more than 500 of his followers at one time, most of whom are still alive, though some have died by now. Then he was seen by James and later by all the apostles. Last of all, I saw him, too, long after the others, as though I had been born at the wrong time.
> — 1 Corinthians 15:3-8 NLT

This is always the basis of a genuine resurrection faith.

A young, ambitious pastor was called to serve in a certain church. He was warned by his predecessor that this congregation was "dead." It was not even worth trying to save. But this pastor accepted the call because he believed with God's guidance he could bring life to that church.

He was an optimist and he worked hard, visiting the members and preaching his best sermons enthusiastically. He tried to develop an outreach of lay visiting program so that visits might be done in the homes of the active, the inactive, and new people moving into town. The harder he tried, the more he knew that his predecessor was right. This was one seriously dead church. It was a shrine for the frozen chosen. It was a mausoleum of faith. There was just nothing there. The spark for ministry, the excitement of sharing the gospel, was just not there. One Sunday he made a startling announcement to the few who were gathered for worship. He said, "Inasmuch as you are a dead congregation, unresponsive to resuscitative efforts, unresponsive to any effort of pumping life into the workings of the congregation, inasmuch as the vital signs of the congregation are dead, I will conduct a funeral for this 'dead' church next Sunday morning at 10:00 am." The members, at least the few who were there, buzzed with excitement following the service. One said, "What's he trying to pull anyway?" Another said, "I don't understand."

The pastor and his announcement of a funeral for the church was the main talk of the tiny rural town during that week. The phone lines were hot with talk. The coffee shop was filled with people talking about what they expected next Sunday. Sunday arrived, and as the people gathered, there was an open coffin in the front of the church. As 10:00 approached, the pastor looked out and saw that every pew plus some chairs were filled for this funeral service. He began the funeral service by reading scripture, he shared prayer, he even gave a very sad sermon on the demise of this over 100-year-old church and congregation. After he finished his sermon, he did something that again startled the membership. He asked the members to please rise and pass slowly by the open coffin to pay their last respects to this dead church. Row by row, the people rose and walked past the coffin. Each of them got the same sheepish, startled look as they scurried quickly away from it. The coffin was empty except for a mirror. As each person peered into the coffin to view the deceased each looked upon his or her own face."[1]

The witness of the apostles comes to us in the witness of scripture. But we never really believe in Jesus solely because of arguments based on their experience. We are assured that he is risen only when we encounter him in our own lives on some personal Emmaus Road of our own. When this happens, we too are filled with great joy and are transformed into evangelist and hope-filled proclaimers of the gospel. When that happens we will never have to look into an empty coffin and find that we are looking at our own image. I don't want to be a part of a dead church, do you?

The closing verses of our reading deserve another proclamation,

> Then Jesus led them to Bethany, and lifting his hands to heaven, he blessed them. While he was blessing them, he left them and was taken up to heaven. They worshiped him and then returned to Jerusalem filled with great joy. And they spent all of their time in the Temple, praising God.
> — Luke 24:50-53 NLT

The image that Luke gives us of Jesus' return to the glory that is heaven calls us individually and corporately to respond. Our response on this day of Ascension should be one of worship filled to fullness with joy and a sense of wonder. Please notice that in our reading there is no more fear, it has been replaced by faith. There is no sense of being lost but rather a sense of being found. There is no sense of confusion about our place in the journey, we are partners as we witness for Christ. All four gospels communicate to us that in the end the disciples were changed. They now had a reason to continue on. Just as they had been filled with pain and sorrow, so now they are filled with faith and hope. They are faith filled followers who have discovered a new and wonderful way to live.

The question for the Christian community on a day such as this is are we or are we not a reflection of the way Jesus wants us to live? If the answer is yes, then we must ask ourselves are we ready to step forward to help others find what we have found. And if the answer is no, then it is time we reexamined our Lenten and Easter journey. The good news is that the journey is ongoing and we are offered all the chances we need to get to where Jesus wants us to be. Amen.

---

1. Educational Ministry "What Does a Dead Church Look Like?" 1989.

A Time Between Time

Today is the last in the season of Eastertide. It has been a wonderful and faith-filled journey as we have traveled from Ash Wednesday through to Maundy Thursday, Good Friday, and Easter. We have participated in a sacred meal, walked the road to Calvary, and been witnesses to the resurrection. It is fitting that today we find our Lord offering an intercessory prayer for his followers.

Luke's gospel tells us that Jesus prayed for his disciples before he even chose them (Luke 6:12), during the time of his active ministry (John 6:12), at the end of his earthly ministry (Luke 22:32). The prayer of intersession found in our reading for today reveals Jesus' loving concern for his apostles.

In the gospel lesson for this day, Jesus prays, and his prayer to God is, "Now I am departing the world; I am leaving them behind and coming to you. Holy Father, keep them and care for them — all those you have given me — so that they will be united just as we are" (John 17:11 NLT). Jesus goes on, "And now I am coming to you. I have told them many things while I was with them so they would be filled with my joy" (John 17:13 NLT), and finally, "And I give myself entirely to you so they also might be entirely yours" (John 17:19 NLT). Jesus' prayer is that the disciples will stay together, that they will find joy in that unity, and consecration will be the result. This united, joyful, consecrated group of disciples will be sent into the world just the way Jesus went into the world. They are the end result of his ministry and the means of his future ministry in the world.

There is an ancient legend that tells of Jesus' ascension into heaven. He is met by the angel Gabriel who asks him, "Now that your work is finished, what plans have you made to insure that the truth you brought to earth will spread throughout the world?"

Jesus answered, "I called some fishermen and tax-collectors to walk along with me as I did my Father's will."

"Yes, I know about them," said Gabriel, "but what other plans have you made?"

Jesus replied, "I taught Peter, James, and John about the kingdom of God; I taught Thomas about faith; and all of them were with me as I healed and preached to the multitudes."

Gabriel began to lose patience. "Really now, all this is well and good, but surely you must have other plans to make sure your work was not in vain."

Jesus fixed Gabriel with a steady gaze and said with finality, "I have no other plans. I am depending on them!"

I wish that I was the one with whom Jesus could always depend but I fear that I am not that strong. I know that I am in need of prayer and I am sure that we all find ourselves standing at the foot of the cross wondering if we would have the courage to even be seen in that place.

Talk about needing help, I think it is fair to say we all do. It is into this kind of human weakness that Jesus offers this wonderful intercessory prayer. And I say into this kind of human weakness because the disciples were after all just human beings with the same kind of frail dispositions that we all possess. Jesus said he was depending on the disciples. He was depending on them to spread the message of love, mercy, and compassion to the entire world. He was depending on them to follow the instructions he gave them when he said in Matthew's gospel, "Therefore, go and make disciples of all the nations, baptizing them in the name of the Father and the Son and the Holy Spirit" (Matthew 28:19 NLT). It is clear that Jesus was depending on the disciples but he would not leave them alone, for he promised them a helper, one who would come in power to give them the needed power to spread his message. Suffice it to say they had no hope without that helper. The disciples knew all of this and they also knew that without Jesus' presence and prayers they would be doomed!

In the church year today is a day of waiting, a time for reflection, a time to stop, to ponder, to listen, to pray, to feel, to experience, to wait, and to wonder.

In the sequence of things, last Thursday was Ascension Day, the day Jesus rose into heaven, and next Sunday is Pentecost, the day when Jesus' Holy Spirit visits the disciples with power. That power birthed what we know as the church of Jesus Christ. This is a time when we as a church are sort of between times.

In a real way the disciples had been separated out of the world. To highlight how important the idea of telling the world about Jesus, the word "world" is used eighteen times in this chapter! The disciples had been chosen to do this work of love and this separation was not by mistake. On the contrary it was by election of the Father, in which the apostles had been given as a gift to Jesus, "However, those the Father has given me will come to me, and I will never reject them" (John 6:37 NLT). The disciples were not perfect, but they had what we would call "the right stuff." Their faith in Jesus was based upon the trust that existed between Jesus and God the Father. This faith was made complete in their obedience to Jesus' words because they believed in his divine mission. Having said that, I imagine the disciples felt frightened, alone, insecure, amazed, and perplexed all at the same time, how human!

They had just seen Jesus rise into heaven. They had just seen their friend, their teacher, their Lord go away from them. This was a glorious event, for now they were certain that Jesus was with the Father, now they knew for sure that Jesus was indeed the Son of God. Now they knew for sure that Jesus and the Father were really one.

On the other hand, now they were alone, now they were without their friend, without their leader, without their companion. Although they were reassured they were also in a kind of limbo. They were sure that Jesus was who he claimed to be but not at all sure about exactly what it was they were to do now. They were in a between times time, almost like being in a dream state, not quite real but real enough that they could not go back to sleep. It was an awkward time for them as they tried to piece together all that Jesus had taught them these past months and years.

Jesus knew that the disciples would now need to step out on their own. He also knew that being alone in ministry for the first time they were going to need help. He had taught them to pray and was now in this prayer asking God to be with them and to give them the courage and perseverance needed in the trying times they would face. It is appropriate that we look at this prayer and keep it in context. Because if the disciples were to think about this text, if they could recall this conservation with Jesus, if they could remember these words, this in between time wouldn't seem so frightening, nor would they seem so alone.

This was Jesus' high priestly prayer. Jesus knew that the hostility against God that had fallen on him would now fall on them. Jesus prayed that God will protect them from those who would do them harm. He prayed for their preservation to promote the unity of the disciples knowing how easy it would be for them to fall into disarray.

It would have been so easy for the disciples to forget all that Jesus had taught them. It would have been easy to say: "Well back to the fishing boats, it's all over. It was good while it lasted, but Jesus is gone, we are alone, there is nothing more for us to do, let's go back to something we know, something with security, something familiar." It would have been very easy for the disciples to have thought this way and who could have blamed them? But if they could remember this prayer of Jesus, they would of have the power, the strength, and the encouragement to wait, to stay in Jerusalem for the coming of the Spirit.

Jesus says, "Now I am departing the world; I am leaving them behind and coming to you. Holy Father, keep them and care for them — all those you have given me — so that they will be united just as we are" (John 17:11 NLT).

Jesus wanted the disciples to have faith, to remain true to the Father, to believe in the promises and teaching he had given them. Jesus knew that in a little while after his ascension, the disciples would have the needed power of the spirit to carry on with his work, so he prays that they would remain true and faithful.

It is like the story of a sailboat that bobbed up and down in the waves as the wind made the trees sway back and forth. The sailboat was clean and smooth, yet it hovered helplessly next to the dock.

The sails danced playfully in the power of the wind, but the boat did not move. Other ships cut across the lake using the wind's silent grace but the boat at the dock did not move. Its sails shook in the wasted breeze. Its hardware rattled and banged with eagerness to be used but the ship drifted helplessly in the windswept water.

All the power was at hand, the wind drenched the boat with its force. The boat was ready but the boat did not move because the person at the tiller did not have the wisdom to use the power and equipment that was available. He did not have the knowledge to set the rigging and did not even know how to direct the craft to receive all the glorious power around it.

The disciples had all the power from Jesus. They had the mission spelled out, they had the tools at hand but they didn't know how to use them yet. They didn't know how to set sail. Once again we see just how like all of us the disciples actually were. The more we look at their lives the more we can see that they were regular folks living in very confusing circumstances.

Remember we always look at biblical history from the side of what has already taken place. They on the other hand do not know what is about to happen. They cannot open their Bibles and see what we can see. They needed what we will celebrate next week and that is the Day of Pentecost. They needed the guidance of the Spirit; they needed the power of the Spirit to get their boat sailing into the wind. Jesus prayed that while they waited for all this, they would be drawn together in one cohesive group and grow strong as they waited to get started in their mission, that they would not lose faith, but they would remain in the Father.

When looked at in its totality, this prayer is really a threefold prayer. Jesus' prayer is, "Now I am departing the world; I am leaving them behind and coming to you. Holy Father, keep them and care for them — all those you have given me — so that they will be united just as we are" (John 17:11). "And now I am coming to you. I have told them many things while I was with them so they would be filled with my joy" (John 17:13) "And I give myself entirely to you so they also might be entirely yours" (John 17:19). That is to say, Jesus' prayer is for their unity, joy, and consecration.

This is the outcome that Jesus desires to see God produce in this the fellowship of believers we call the apostles. It is none other than the unity that exists in the Father and the Son, the joy the Son himself has in the love of the Father, and the consecration that comes through knowing the Son who is the truth. This united, joyful, consecrated group is to be sent forth into the world even as Jesus was sent into the world. It is the product of his ministry and the means of his future ministry, through which Jesus himself is to do the greater works.

There is something we can learn from this text and sequence of events, too. Jesus also prays for us to remain in the faith as we face the in between times of our lives.

Like the disciples there are many times when you and I are not quite sure of our faith, not quite sure what is going to happen next, not quite sure what the future is going to hold for us. It is appropriate for us to know that even when we are confused, even if we don't know what is going to happen, even if we cannot get our boat sailing, we still have a relationship with Jesus. We still have faith. We can cling to his promises and we can rely on his redemption in our lives. We might feel in between but Jesus is still there for us to fill in the gaps.

In this in-between time for the disciples, Jesus' words are directing them to the Father's words, to the Father's teaching, to Jesus' teaching to make them holy. It gives them something to turn to, gives them something to rely on, and it gives them something on which to hold. As we face our in-between times, and also our everyday living, we know that Jesus is praying for us to remain in faith and remain in the truth of God's word.

We thank him for those prayers and we pray that he will give us the power to be faithful to him and to his words as we look forward to the Day of Pentecost, another day of celebration and hope! Amen.